THE WHOLE FROMAGE

COLLECTION MANAGEMENT

BROADWAY PAPERBACKS

NEW YORK

THE

WHOLE

FROMAGE

ADVENTURES IN THE
DELECTABLE WORLD OF
FRENCH CHEESE

KATHE LISON

BROADWAY

BROADWAY BOOKS and the Broadway Books colophon
are trademarks of Random House, Inc.

Library of Congress Cataloging-in-Publication Data
Lison, Kathe.
The whole fromage: adventures in the delectable world of French cheese /
Kathe Lison.
1. Cheese—France—History. 2. Cheese—Varieties—France. 3. Lison, Kathe—
Travel—France. I. Title.
SF274.F7L57 2013
637'.350944—dc23   2012045290

ISBN 978-0-307-45206-1
eISBN 978-0-307-45207-8

PRINTED IN THE UNITED STATES OF AMERICA

Map by Meredith Hamilton
Cover design by Elena Giavaldi
Cover photography: Julian Winslow/Gallerystock

1 3 5 7 9 10 8 6 4 2

First Edition

For Chris, who once said to me,
"You could write a book about French cheese!"

"Like a Brie ripened to its heart, the lover of cheeses is also the product of a long and delicate aging."

—JAMES DE COQUET

CONTENTS

FRANCE
A Story of Fromage

Maroilles.

Isigny-sur-Mer.
Ferme de la Héronnière..
Vimoutiers
.Paris
Camembert

Loire River
Valençay
Époisses
.Langres
Jura
Poligny. .St. Antoine

Buron d'Algour
Annecy. .Beaufort-sur-Doron

Ferme de Poutignac.
.!.Salers
Alpage de Bellachat

La Borie d'Imbert. .Rocamadour
Massif
Central
Alps

Roquefort-sur-Soulzon.

Bedous. Pyrenees
.Cabane de
René Miramon

A CHEESEHEAD
CONFRONTS PARADISE

~~~~~~~~~~~~~~

"The French are sawed-off sissies who eat snails and slugs and
cheese that smells like people's feet."

—P. J. O'ROURKE

The blade of Napoleon's sword scythed air redolent of
roasted meat as the man who would one day be emperor
severed the top of the cheese before him. Its point landed with
a soft plop. Moments earlier, Charles-Maurice de Talleyrand-
Périgord, renowned French diplomat and the owner of the
Château de Valençay, had noted the scowl creeping across the
general's face. The stain of red on his cheeks had nothing to do
with their recent scorching by an Egyptian sun, nor the warm
breezes wafting through from doors flung open to a gravel

courtyard. Inside the room, a hush fell over the guests gathered around the mahogany table, the silver-plate carving stand, the china banded in moss green and gilt. Outside, below the courtyard, the Nahon River, one of the numerous tributaries whose waters eventually join the Loire, flowed in a quiet, dark streak.

Not long before, France had triumphed at the Battle of the Pyramids, and the success of Napoleon's North African campaign seemed assured. Back then, Talleyrand had relished the pyramid-shaped *fromage* produced on nearby farms. Why had he, Talleyrand, so skilled in the art of subtle manipulation, not considered how Napoleon might feel about the cheese now that the general had returned in defeat? The sound of the courtyard fountain, its spout ringed by cherubic stone children, trickled into the silence; a wine bottle, nestled in one of two marble basins attached to the walls, shifted with a dull clunk. The guests, many of whom had jumped from their seats when the general called for his sword, stood without moving. Encumbered by the brace he wore for a chronic limp, Talleyrand remained near his chair, the froth of lace at his throat quivering. Napoleon spared none of them a glance as he set the sword next to the serving plate, nabbed a morsel of the now-decapitated cheese, and chewed.

This is one account—shamelessly embellished—of how the goat cheese known as Valençay came to be shaped like a flattened pyramid. Other stories have Talleyrand beheading the cheese; in still others, the peasants around Valençay do the deed. According to yet another variation, Talleyrand, wanting to enjoy the fine goat cheese from his country estate while in Paris, ordered his steward to alter the cheese molds before sending the tasty *chèvres* to the city, where the emperor might see them. But the most popular version is the one in which Napoleon himself lops the tip off—a story with a heady mix of celebrity, defiant Frenchness, a hint of danger, and of course, a dash of cheese.

MY OWN STORY with French cheese began less dramatically, with a trip to Paris. Charles de Gaulle is supposed to have said, "How can anyone govern a country that has 246 different kinds of cheese?" But de Gaulle's number was only one estimate, as the book I bought one Christmas Eve at Charles de Gaulle Airport made clear: a Dorling Kindersley "visual guide to more than 350 cheeses from every region of France." Though I didn't realize it at the time, the actual number of French cheeses is one of those great unknowables, like the place the other sock disappeared to or whether or not God exists. Even the ubiquitous de Gaulle quote doesn't stay constant—sometimes he laments the existence of 258 cheeses, sometimes 227, sometimes 324. Other sources say it wasn't even de Gaulle but rather Winston Churchill who wanted to know "How can you govern a country with over 300 cheeses?"—to which the French president supposedly snapped back, "There are at least 350." This number at least squares with that of my guidebook, but falls far short of estimates that put the number of French cheeses as high as 650. Six hundred and fifty. Cheeses. All produced in a country smaller than Texas.

I'd bought the book to learn more about the cheeses that my partner, Chris, and I were smuggling out of the country in our suitcases. One of them, a pungent, gooey cow's-milk cheese from the French Jura called Vacherin Mont d'Or, qualified as contraband: a raw-milk cheese—i.e., an unpasteurized one—aged fewer than sixty days. Completely illegal in the United States, though at the time it didn't occur that something as innocuous-seeming as cheese could turn us into petty criminals. The cheese was cushioned in a suit newly bought for Chris; he was making elaborate plans for fumigation even before we left French soil. When I showed him the book, Chris took one look at the cover and said, "Three hundred and fifty cheeses! That's practically a different cheese for every day of the year."

"I know," I responded, nearly whispering in awe, before plunking into a chair near our gate.

I opened the book—and encountered pictures so vivid I had to resist an urge to press my nose to the pages to see if I could smell them. There were cheeses with wild mulberry leaves pressed into their tops; cheeses bound with rushes; cheeses covered in ash, in cumin, in raisins, in bits of grape skin; cheeses furred with long hairs of mold; cheeses in the shape of bricks, logs, bells, sheep turds; gigantic round cheeses that could crush a poodle; and tiny goat cheeses so tender-looking you wanted to pick them up and soothe them. As I turned each glossy page, revealing another and yet another fabulous, even fantastical, cheese, I began to have questions. Why produce this crazy number of cheeses? I mean, why not just one nice sharp cheddar? The French, I would eventually discover, have so many cheeses and so much lore to go with them that there's even a *Larousse des fromages*—a French cheese encyclopedia. What was the deal with the French and all this *fromage*? I wanted to find out.

GIVEN MY UPBRINGING, you might say my interest in cheese was inevitable. I confess: I am a Cheesehead. By this, I don't just mean that I love cheese (though, I do) or that I have a cheese obsession (though, I suppose you could say that), but that I was born and raised in Green Bay, Wisconsin, the place where otherwise sane-seeming folk regularly don foam wedges shaped like giant slices of Gruyère (though colored a bizarre, alien yellow we can only hope real Gruyère never attains). On Packer Sundays, these wedges crown the heads of the faithful at Lambeau Field, one part of a football, beer, and cheese-bratwurst trifecta.

When it comes to cheese, people from Wisconsin just can't help themselves. License plates proclaim the state "America's Dairyland," and picture a happy little red barn, happy little flapping birds, and a happy orange sunset. Some people believe that Colby, invented in Colby, Wisconsin, may have been the first truly American cheese. Wisconsin is the nation's largest producer of cheese, although California has long been on its tail, a fact that pisses off Wisconsinites to no end. A *New York Times* report outlining the looming takeover quoted various cheese people in my home state: "Say cheese and you say Wisconsin," claimed one. "When you drive through Wisconsin, what do you see but cheese? It's who we are," said another. As one journalist put it, "Cheese is a kind of secular religion in the upper Midwest, particularly in Wisconsin."

My maternal grandfather kept and milked a dozen Holsteins on a farm north of Green Bay, and on my father's side, my great-great-grandfather started a dairy that remained in the family well into the 1960s; as a boy, my grandfather rode along in the milk wagon making deliveries. In my kitchen sits an old bottle, the words "Lison's Dairy" scrolling across its front in brown letters. I heard about that mom-and-pop operation—the empty storefront was a few blocks from my grandparents' Green Bay home—all the time as I was growing up: "You should have tasted their chocolate milk!" As far as I know, no one in the family made cheese themselves, but my progenitors were certainly up to their eyeballs in udders.

Still, the Wisconsin cheese I ate in the 1970s could hardly be considered "artisanal." Even if such cheeses had been available, I was the trailer park kid of a single mother just scraping by, sometimes with the help of food stamps. The cheese we knew was a somewhat bland, orange variety that came from the local food pantry in brown cardboard boxes stamped "U.S.D.A.," or the sort found in Kraft Macaroni & Cheese—which, to be technical, is not really cheese at all. Mom used to pull a chair up to the stove and let me stir the elbow noodles, then help add the milk, butter, and garish powder that made the mess a cheesy delight. Many of my organic-only, low-fat, health nut friends are horrified when I own that even now, as an adult, I still eat Kraft Mac & Cheese. I have upgraded to the more refined "Three Cheese with Mini-Shell Pasta" version, but it comes in that same blue box, an old pal on the cupboard shelf.

In other words, my childhood cheese, like that of most Americans, was industrial cheese. All of it was a far cry from raw-milk cheeses made high in the French Alps in wee chalets where they've been making cheese for centuries, or from cheeses with marvelous crusty rinds the color of toast, or from still others that you can break into and eat with a spoon. Wisconsin might be really into cheese, but it doesn't come close to rivaling France—a fact I largely ignored when I spent a semester in Paris during my early twenties. Back then, in my fresh-from-the-Midwest naïveté, I thought even *chèvre* suspect—who on earth had ever heard of cheese made with milk from a *goat?*— and ate tiny Babybel cheeses on butter-smeared baguettes. I thought Babybel—a mild, white, processed cheese that could be considered the French equivalent of a plastic-wrapped slice of American—the most marvelous cheese ever. Now most of us can likely find Babybel at our local supermarket, but back then, it was exotic—it was French!—and I munched away happily at my Babybel sandwiches in various Parisian locales, trying to affect an authentic air. Yet I remained ignorant. That much was obvious as I stood in Charles de Gaulle Airport nearly a decade later holding a book full of cheeses I knew nothing about.

CERTAINLY I'M NOT the first American to be smitten by French cheese. Americans have been coveting *fromage* at least since the middle of the nineteenth century; we began importing Roquefort in the 1830s and '40s, and by the late 1880s were bringing it in at a rate of five million kilos a year. Even so, it's only in the past three or four decades—as more and more Americans have traveled to France and had the opportunity to taste the local specialties—that we've developed a serious craving for it. The publication of two books in particular helped to intensify this hunger. The first was *Le guide du fromage,* published in the States in 1973 as *The Complete Encyclopedia of French Cheese.* The author was Pierre Androuët, the proprietor of a huge handlebar mustache and an international cheese superstar, the "pope" of French cheese. "Pierre Androuët invented everything," recalled French cheesemonger Hervé Mons in 2005, shortly after Androuët's death. "He opened the way, showed the path. [. . .]. He was one of those visionary men like Edouard Michelin, who wasn't content merely to sell tires, but thought about everything that went along with that: road maps, good restaurants, the necessity of customer service [. . .]." Though one might argue that Pierre's father, Henri—who founded La Maison Androuët at 41 rue d'Amsterdam in Paris, one of the greatest temples to *fromage* that has ever existed—was the real visionary, the point about Pierre Androuët is well made. For Americans who knew little about French cheese, Androuët's work demystified a number of previously impenetrable *fromages,* and whet our appetites for more than Velveeta.

The other book was written by the monocled, irascible, and very British figure of Patrick Rance. At a bend in the road in the village of Streatley, an hour or so outside of London, you can still see the hobbit-size redbrick storefront out of which he famously sold hundreds of different cheeses alongside dog food and shoelaces. Unlike Androuët, who set out to create gastronomic legend, Rance was more of a cheese hobbyist whose passions had run amok. Having sparked a renaissance in British farmhouse cheese with his store, he next bought a house in Provence and embarked on six years of travel across France in order to write *The French Cheese Book,* which appeared in 1989. In it, he actually catalogues more than 650 types of *fromage*—stopping around 750. "I should have liked to produce a more comprehensive book," he writes mournfully, "but life is too short." Pierre Androuët himself called Rance's exhaustive guide "the best of all," and it remains one of the definitive texts on French cheese.

Androuët's work, coming at the beginning of the 1970s, signaled the start of a profound shift in the American cheese scene. In his 1976 book *The World of Cheese,* Evan Jones—husband to

Judith Jones, the editor who discovered Julia Child—wrote of a proliferation of Parisian-style cheese shops across America. This might have been mostly wishful thinking on Jones's part; I myself don't recall seeing so much as Brie or Camembert in anyone's house until the 1980s or '90s, and then it was the awful, bland deception foisted on the American public by makers such as Président. Still, those sad, oven-warmed Bries signaled brewing change. In New York, cheesemongers such as Rob Kaufelt of Murray's Cheese Shop and Steven Jenkins of Fairway—Rance's encyclopedic volume in hand—were importing more French varieties than most Americans had ever imagined existed. By 2004, Cynthia Zarin was writing in *The New Yorker* about cheese as a cultural happening: "In the past few years, the cheese landscape in New York—what kind of cheese you can buy, who makes it, who's eating it, and where—has changed dramatically; it's like the moment when black-and-white TV turned into full-spectrum color." The days when wine-soaked balls covered in sliced almonds were the height of American cheese sophistication were quickly becoming a memory.

Some of these cheeses, of course, were British or Italian or Spanish. But most of them were French. "There is nowhere like France when it comes to cheese," writes Liz Thorpe, formerly of Murray's, the celebrated New York cheese store. "The French make the fluffy, the sexy, the drippy, the runny, the delicate, the stoic, the [entire] crumbling, hulking, racy, lacy, oozing spectrum . . ." France, she concludes, "is the Cheese Mother Ship."

And if the past several decades are any indication, we Americans would like nothing better than to be beamed aboard.

Our newfound enthusiasm for artisanal cheeses, however, remains tempered by a certain amount of consternation. The French are used to the many alien forms that curdled milk can assume—I once watched a group of French truckers tuck matter-of-factly into a platter of gooey cheeses that would have sent their Stateside counterparts running. We Americans, however, sometimes get a little rattled when forced out of our Monterey Jack comfort zone. Not only is the world of *fromage* filled with hunks of things that smell like armpits or come covered in green crusties, but there's also the sheer number of French cheeses to contend with. I'd thought my impulse purchase from the airport bookstore would help me to master this strange new world, but as my questions multiplied, I realized I'd underestimated my subject.

And I realized typologies and glossy pictures would take me only so far. Not only that, but what I truly yearned for was a different, more intimate kind of knowledge. I wanted to see where the cheeses came from, talk with the people who made them, lift the cheeses from the often stultifying pages of "gourmet" guides, replete with tips on where to stick them on a serving plate. I wanted them to come alive. For cheese *is* alive. Cheeses breathe; they evolve, gain complexity; they peak. They can be mishandled—even killed. (As Pierre Androuët warns, "Never put them in the freezer. That would be an act of murder.")

The only thing for it was to leave the guidebooks behind, and so I set off into the "wilds" of the French countryside. There, I quickly discovered the delights of going where the *fromage* takes you. Study a map of France, and you'll find that cheeses—often named after the hamlet from which they came—are part of the very warp and weft of the country. Following them led me to places I never would have visited were it not for a dot labeled "Maroilles" or "Langres." Zigzagging my way across *la France profonde* from one such locale to the next, I logged more than 6,800 miles, and very likely ate my weight in artisanal French *fromage*. Along the way, I met scores of wonderful cheesemakers who introduced me to oodles of extraordinary cheeses.

From that bounty, I have chosen a handful of makers and cheeses, selecting them in part because they represent the basic cheese categories produced in France. More and more, such knowledge comes in handy not only when it comes to sorting out French cheeses, but also American ones. For not long after we began importing European offerings by the cartload, some began wondering if we couldn't make such cheeses ourselves. Soon enough, makers on this side of the Atlantic began churning out record numbers of piquant, crusty cheeses of their own. Many of these "new" American cheeses now poking aromatic heads from market stalls across the country are, of course, interpretations or outright imitations of cheeses birthed in an obscure French village centuries ago.

Take, for example, a cheese called Thistle Hill Farm Tarentaise, which looks like the baby cousin of the Alpine cheese Beaufort, and is named after French Tarentaise cows. Or Jasper Hill Farm Winnimere, a billowy circle girdled by a strip of spruce bark, made in Vermont but modeled on Mont d'Or. Or the handmade, raw-milk *tomme* made just up the road from where I used to live in tiny Logan, Utah. Even our good old American cheese balls have a French original: Gaperon, a spherical *fromage* from central France.

Once upon a time, it's said, young men judged the size of a farm girl's dowry by the number of cheesy Gaperon orbs that hung curing by the family fire. The fairy-tale aura of this tale hints at an even more elemental fact that the cheeses in this book make plain: Cheese is more than mere food. This is doubly true if you are French. Androuët famously called cheese "the soul of the soil," and you can hold it crumbling in your hands, solid and real, like earth. This is why Michelin starred restaurants in Paris parade cheese platters around their dining rooms: They're not just cheeses; they're living morsels of *la campagne* itself. It also explains why when leftist politician Ségolène Royal dressed as a peasant and got the French National Assembly to serenade Chabichou, a goat cheese from her native region of Poitou (as part of a campaign to get the cheese's name legally protected), she became an instant political star. If Scarlett O'Hara had been French, no doubt she would have held up a sliver of cheese rather than the dirt of Tara when she vowed never to be hungry again.

Nor do the metaphors stop there. Hang around eating cheese

with a French person for more than five minutes and someone is likely to quote the famed gastronome Brillat-Savarin: "A meal without some cheese is like a beautiful woman with only one eye." Skip the *fromage,* that is, and you're not just disfigured but half blind. Cheese thus becomes a way of seeing, a way of knowing not only who the French are, but where they came from. As Patrick Rance once put it, "A slice of cheese is never just a thing to eat, it is also a slice of history." Contained within that history are vital questions about food culture, how you go about maintaining it, and why you should even bother. "Food history," writes Carlo Petrini, a founder of the tradition-promoting Slow Food movement, "is as important as a baroque church, a cheese is as worthy of preserving as a sixteenth-century building."

There's certainly no shortage of food history to preserve when it comes to French cheese. Over the centuries, it has kept infants from starving, served as currency, shaped landscapes, helped to disseminate religion, inspired poetry, sparked protests, and started wars (well, cheese wars). This is why we love cheese: It contains multitudes. Nevertheless, keeping cheese history is not as easy as it may appear. Unlike a cathedral, after all, cheese is alive.

So, too, are the ways of making a cheese. This is where artisanal French cheesemaking gets rather, well, sticky. Through the beginning of the twentieth century, most of French cheesemaking continued on rather placidly as it always had done. Innovations emerged in an organic way from the lives and surroundings of the makers. The modern era, however, brought unprecedented changes (what traditional French peasant, after all, could ever have envisioned the invention of cheese you can spray from a can?). These changes would utterly transform French cheese, challenging the way the French—and by extension, food lovers across the globe—think about cheese. Today "defenders" of French cheese abound, all claiming to know what "tradition" means, how that tradition ought to be kept, and who ought to keep it. We don't often think of cheese as worthy of battle, yet the story of nearly every French *fromage* is a story of struggle—for the cheese, yes, but also for a way of life.

THERE'S AN EXPRESSION in French *"en faire tout un fromage."* If you make a cheese of something, that is, you've made a big deal from next to nothing. Though the saying isn't necessarily a compliment (the closest English equivalent might be to "make a mountain of a molehill"), it nevertheless strikes me as an apt description of all that French cheese contains. As I made my way across the French countryside, more than one cheesemaker would press a wedge of cheese wrapped in paper into my hands as we parted. The cheese was a gift. A gift of their land, their animals, their labor, and their sometimes complicated *fromage* histories. It was a story of them that becomes a story of French cheese that becomes something more. A vivid and far richer story than I could possibly have imagined that day in the airport as I sat flipping through pictures in a guidebook. It was, you might say, a story that makes a cheese out of cheese.

1

DREAM A LITTLE DREAM OF CHEESE

~~~~~~~~~~~~~

"Never commit yourself to a cheese without having
first examined it."

—T. S. ELIOT

If I were going to own a cow, it would be a Salers. I'd name
her Lulabelle, and she would have a curling coat of auburn
hair that spread along her sides in whorls. I would brush it every
morning, all the way through to her corkscrew tail, so that
in the sunlight it would look like burnished copper. Lulabelle
and I would go for long walks, and if we ever got separated,
I wouldn't have to worry, because in a storm, Salers cows are
smart enough to ring their bells so their owners can find them.
I'd have a stall built in the backyard, one that would be big
enough for her calf, too. Because no matter how much Lulabelle

and I might love one another, if I wanted to milk her, I'd have to let her calf suckle first. It's not that Lulabelle would mean to hurt my feelings—some breeds are just that way. "*Un travail de dingue*" is what people in the Cantal *département* of Auvergne say about milking Salers cows. They mean that to milk a Salers, you have to be a nutcase.

Certainly you have to get out of bed early. It was 5:30 as I plodded down a long, muddy red-dirt driveway on a mountain in the middle of France. I'd left my hotel in the nearby village of Salers under a sky still drizzly with stars, turning off the highway and onto a gravel side road so slippery it felt as though I were picking my way upward over ice. I was there because I'd heard that in Auvergne, there were cheesemakers who not only still kept whole herds of Salers cows, but also still milked those herds twice a day *à la main*—"by hand."

Hand-milking is one of those things that cheese connoisseurs find really attractive. As American cheese man Max McCalman writes, "There is really no substitute for doing it the old-fashioned way." He warns that using machines can lead to mastitis, an infection of the udder. Though he doesn't come out and say that cheesemakers shouldn't use milking machines, the implication is that the best cheeses are made by individuals who eschew modern ways, those willing to do the work that others, with their newfangled gadgets, skip. Good cheese requires a certain amount of hard labor—a certain quotient of sweat, a willingness to suffer.

And yet even in France, and even among those who hew to

the old ways, hand-milking your cows (let alone a bunch of Salers cows) is considered taking things rather far. As a result, a true milking *à la main* has a faintly sacred aura, and I imagined that watching one might feel rather like getting sprinkled with holy water. As I walked, the jangle and chime of cowbells broke the predawn stillness. They might not have been church bells, but the sound of a herd of bell-clad cows is perhaps even more ethereal: something you'd like to package up and unwrap back at home where it could linger above your days. A gentle curve of land bowed the dirt track I followed, and grassy knolls studded with wildflowers still gray in the early light stretched away on both sides. Ahead I could make out the dim shapes of the cows to which the bells were attached. Somewhere among them was Guy Chambon, the man I was hoping just might be one of the nutcases.

AUVERGNE HAS ALWAYS been a curious sort of place. It lies across the northern part of the Massif Central, the wedge-shaped collection of hills and low mountains that dominate central France. Even though, geographically, Auvergne is at the core of the country, it's traditionally been so isolated and forbidding that guidebooks tend to omit it altogether. Go to Normandy, to Paris, to the Southwest, to Provence, to the Côte d'Azur, they seem to urge, but whatever you do, don't head in. Parts of the area reminded me oddly of Upper Michigan—pine trees and more pine trees, broken here and there by little grass-filled clearings—only then I'd round a curve and see stubby peaks stippling the horizon, the remnants of volcanoes active millions of years earlier. The volcanoes left huge circular cones in the land that the French call *puys*. Around Salers, where the *puys* are older, they look like ordinary mountains from the ground, but aerial images of their huge, circular rims stare from the postcard racks of every souvenir shop in the region. They're supposed to be scenic, yet at the same time they're a reminder that upheaval is in Auvergne's very ground. I saw more crosses there than anywhere else in France, popping out of farm fields, on pedestals along roadways, on the tops of stony hills—as if the people living on that land felt the only thing to do was stick a symbol of their hope for salvation in it and pray. Dwellings were traditionally built from the granite and basalt and gneiss scattered in the eruptions, and sometimes people constructed houses and even whole villages out of caves formed from consolidated volcanic ash, also known as tuff. People still put cheeses in *caves* of tuff, where they age among rocks that once, long ago, were on fire.

Historically speaking, the natives haven't exactly been known for their hospitality. In the 1700s a cartographer trying to survey the land was hacked to death by villagers suspicious of the strange instruments he carried, and one nineteenth-century geographer advised travelers to make observations of the region by hot-air balloon, though "only if the aeronaut can remain out of range of a rifle." One of the region's big specialties, besides cheese, was knives, and even today you can usually find at least one shop window stocked with shiny blades in nearly every village. Modern Auvergnats are a friendlier lot than their predecessors—the owner of my hotel in Salers went so far as personally to wash mud and cow muck off my tennis shoes with his garden hose—but you still feel an undertow of deep recalcitrance. One time, I watched a young man running across a pasture yelling *"Allez!"*as he helped a woman corral seven or eight Salers cows, all of them protesting in the loud, trumpet-like way that cows do when prodded: "Moo-wa-A! Moooo-WAAA-A!" The sun was going down, and slanting, honeyed rays illuminated his punked-out, bleach-blond hair, biker boots, and the razor-edged letters that spelled out "Metallica" across his chest. If I were going to pick a scene to represent Auvergne—modern and unruly and yet somehow pastoral—it would be that one. I've seen the region referred to as the "belly button" of France, but it's closer to say it's the entrails. This is where the guts of France lie, coiled around the volcanic hills. If the authentic is going to endure in France, chances are good it endures in Auvergne.

FEW THINGS COULD be more authentic in Auvergne than a family of cylindrical mountain cheeses known as *fourmes*. All *fourmes* bear an uncanny resemblance to a beer barrel, but some are so small they look like miniature pony kegs, while others are remarkably large, weighing upward of 110 pounds. (Even in Wisconsin, that would be a lot of beer.) Their documented history stretches back some two thousand years—Pliny the Elder mentions a cheese thought to be their ancestor. *Fourmes* go by several names: The ones made around the town of Laguiole, for example, are called Laguiole. The cheeses made around the village of Salers with Salers cows used to be called Salers, but somehow people gradually started calling them "Cantal," after the *département* in which Salers is located. The *département,* in turn, is named for the Monts du Cantal, yet another ring of ancient volcanoes.

If they had enough milk, people in the old days sometimes made large *fourmes* on their farms, but the traditional place to make a big cheese was in the mountains, where herders took their animals to graze and live during the warm months. This seasonal migration is properly known as *la transhumance,* from the Latin *trans,* meaning "across," and *humus,* meaning "ground." Throughout the mountainous regions of Western Europe, people have *transhumed* their herds pretty much for as long as they've had domesticated animals, leading them to higher elevations, where lush grasses and forbs grow during the summer, while giving the lower pastures a chance to rejuvenate. Some *transhumance* routes are quite short, just a few miles from the valley to, say, the peaks above the village; while others, like those connecting low-lying settlements in Provence to the Alpine regions, can stretch for tens of miles and took weeks to complete. For millennia, people walked these routes alongside their beasts, and from the air, some of the paths they trod can still be made out, etched into the land like veins.

Different regions gave different names to the high summer pastures—in Auvergne, they're typically called *estives*. No matter the region, summers in the mountains were hard. The day's work began before the sun had begun to glow in the east. Milking could take several hours, and once it was done, there was a first round of cheesemaking, which also took several hours. A quick break for lunch, and the cheesemaker might have time to tend to a few sick or injured animals before the second milking in the evening, followed by the second round of cheesemaking. If he was lucky, he might finish by eight or so at night, leaving enough time for a late supper before bed, usually around ten o'clock. And then it was up before dawn the following morning to do it all over again. And again. And again. Seven days a week, morning and night, for the entire season.

In the *estives* of Auvergne, cheesemakers lived in what was called a *buron,* a long, low shelter built of fieldstone that looked something like a miniature barn. Very little of Auvergne is flat; everywhere you go the land is either falling away or rising up. Some of these slopes are forested, but *estives* were located on bare, treeless expanses, places where there's nothing but the geometry of raw, green curves spread against the sky. *Burons* were often built into the side of one of these mounds—the better to make a cheese *cave*—and had slanting roofs that nearly met the ground, so that they looked as though they were trying to tuck themselves into the earth.

Living in one bore a marked resemblance to camping, with a sleeping mat of straw on a wooden frame in a small attic above the cheesemaking room, and cooking utensils sitting alongside cheesemaking tools on shelves near the hearth. Through the mid-twentieth century, most *burons* had no central heat, no electricity, and no phone. People cooked on an open flame, used lanterns for light, and kept warm as best they could. These were spartan little cheese outposts, shelters pulled up out of the earth stone by stone, rife with cracks and leaks, and smelling dankly of rock.

When the weather was good, life there could be lovely—if laborious. And it could bring in a good living, good enough that at the start of the twentieth century there were still a thousand or so *burons* in operation. As time went on, however, it became harder and harder to find men willing to spend three or four months of the year tending animals and making cheese in a stone hut in the middle of nowhere. And the modern era ushered in new and increasingly stringent sanitary regulations for cheesemaking. This meant renovations that might be not only costly, but also difficult to implement, given the remoteness of most *buron* locations. Little by little, the *burons* were slowly abandoned. Today fewer than a half dozen still make cheese. The ruins of the old ones can still be seen here and there in the high pastures of Auvergne, where they sit quietly crumbling back into the stony ground from which they came.

AS PEOPLE STOPPED going to the *burons,* they started making more and more cheese on their farms. Then they started making it in dairies. Then they started shortening aging times and making it with pasteurized milk, until by the 1950s, larger and larger operations were churning out more and more rounds of really boring Cantal. But there were a few holdouts—people who continued to go each summer to the mountains to make what they called *Cantal de haute montagne*. These makers objected to their cheeses being lumped in with the bland, factory ones. To solve the problem, they petitioned the French government to create a special *Appellation d'Origine Contrôlée*—an AOC, or name-control designation—for their cheese. In 1961 the AOC was granted, and the cheeses were given the old name of Salers.

In appearance, Salers is indistinguishable from Cantal; it's as if the two cheeses were identical twins separated at birth. One struggled in a bad environment, while the other, raised down the road (or up the mountain, as the case may be), had a different life entirely. Salers cheese is special because it's the only traditional French cheese that cannot be made in a factory or in a small dairy. Its production is exclusively *fermier*—what we would call "farmhouse." To give an idea of how scarce such cheese is, consider that a few years ago all the Salers makers together produced 1,400 tons of cheese. Compare that with 17,000 tons of Cantal. Even in France, Salers is a connoisseur's *fromage*; most ordinary French people I talked to had never even heard of it.

But the rules don't say you have to make Salers in a *buron*—there are far too few *burons* left for that—so most Salers these days is made on farms. You don't even have to have an entire herd of Salers cows; makers of the cheese are allowed to mix their herds. And you certainly don't have to milk your cows by hand. The *burons* that remain in operation, then, are one of the few, very few places where you can still see cheesemaking done entirely by hand from start to finish, in a completely authentic way. In 2006, American cheese expert Liz Thorpe visited one of these last working *burons*. She wrote of the owner, Marcel Taillé, who rose "in the dark and the cold" because "the milk must be gathered by hand." She described how he and his helpers made their bleary-eyed way to the cows each morning, "one-legged stools bound to their waists so they can rock back in balance as they squat under the udders." Once they'd finished the task, they strapped their full milk barrels to a cart, pulled by nothing less than "a blind and ancient donkey" from the pastures. "One slap of the flank," she wrote, "and the donkey, unaided, winds his way back to the cheesemaking room. He has made the same trip each day, all summer long, for fifteen years."

Thorpe explained that the only reason the Taillé *buron* had survived at all was through the support of Hervé Mons. Mons is a third-generation *affineur*—a "cheese ager." Some cheesemakers—*fromagers* in French (or *fromagères,* if they're women)—age their own cheese, but others hand over part or all of the task to someone such as Mons. Mons doesn't actually make cheese himself. Instead, following the model originated by Parisian father-and-son cheesemongers Henri and Pierre Androuët, he goes out and finds the best makers he can and brings their cheeses back to coax them into ripeness in his *cave*. Mons is so good that he's earned a Meilleur Ouvrier de France—"Master Craftsman of France"—medal doing this. Like all truly great *affineurs,* however, he coaxes along more than mold. Henri Androuët, working in the first half of the twentieth century, was well known not only for telling cheesemakers how to better their product, but also for coming up with clever ways to broaden a cheese's appeal. The most famous example of this is a triple cream (i.e., a cheese containing over 75 percent butterfat) that saw stardom in the 1930s after he dubbed it "Brillat Savarin." Mons is so well known on not only the French cheese scene, but also the American one, that a few years ago Whole Foods inked a deal with him to supply its stores with traditional Camembert cheeses printed with the words "selected by Hervé Mons." The pressure to live up to past successes might explain why Mons is a tad manic—according to Thorpe, he never sleeps more than four hours a night and likes to take "endless hairpin turns at 130 kilometers an hour." When I called him on the phone, he spoke such rapid-fire French that I wasn't sure how he was managing to breathe and talk at the same time.

Mons was the natural choice, then, for a guide when the makers of a documentary about French cheese called *Ces fromages qu'on assassine—The Assassinated Cheeses*—decided to visit a *buron*. The film, which was rebroadcast over and over on French television, is partly inspired by the Franco-American documentary *Mondovino*, which portrays a band of noble traditional

French winemakers struggling against diabolical, large-scale, mostly California-based multinational producers. In *The Assassinated Cheeses*, Périco Légasse, a food columnist for the far-left-leaning magazine *Marianne,* stars as "The Expert," while a young Swedish man, Erik Svensson, plays the "Apprentice Gastronome." Légasse is a bilious man of some girth, with salt-and-pepper hair, a dark mustache, and a permanent "man-scaped" five-o'clock shadow darkening his jowls; he's somehow Napoleonic in bearing, only fatter. Svensson, on the other hand, is a twentysomething who manages to meld the lankiness of a colt with the eagerness of a puppy as he runs around saying things such as "*Oui, Chef*"—"Yes, Boss"—whenever Légasse tells him to do something.

Together the two set off from Paris into the countryside in an RV—the filmmakers having decided to structure the action around the curiously American trope of a road trip. Recreational-type vehicles may have been in use in Europe for centuries in the form of gypsy caravans, but there's still something incongruous about a Frenchman bellying up to the wheel of one as if preparing to set out for Yosemite with the wife and kids. You almost expect to see Légasse popping the lid on a can of Coke or tearing into a bag of Doritos as they take off. But this is France, and as they pull away from Paris, Légasse is telling Svensson that there's a crisis in traditional French cheese: a *"crise autour du lait cru."*

The crisis, that is, revolves around raw milk. If cheese is the metaphorical soul of the soil, then raw milk—*lait cru*—is how the soul travels from the earth to the plants, through the cow, and into the cheese. Raw-milk cheese is cheese in its highest expression. The problem, Légasse explains to Svensson, is that consumption of *fromages au lait cru* continues to tumble in France. Consumers simply don't care enough about their own cheese heritage.

And so as the RV snails its way through the verdant hills of Auvergne, Légasse says they're going to see the "AOC of AOCs, *le nec plus ultra, le top*" of French cheesemaking, meaning Salers. They arrive at Marcel Taillé's *buron,* where they're greeted by Mons. Like Thorpe before them, Légasse and Svensson watch as the milkers sit on their one-legged stools, milking away into pails. "It's very beautiful," Légasse comments as the workers' strong hands pull. "Very impressive." The camera lingers on a set of udders, milk squirting and frothing, and Légasse calls to Svensson, "Look! It's admirable. And it's endured like that for centuries."

"It's always been like that," Mons agrees, looking on.

After the milking is done, Légasse asks for a taste, and then they all quaff raw milk straight from the pail as if it were mead laced with ambrosia.

BY THE TIME I found myself walking in the semi-dark along the muddy lane toward Guy Chambon's Buron d'Algour, I'd been trying off and on to track down a suitable *buron* for over a year.

In general, I hadn't been having a whole lot of luck with *burons,* even the nonworking ones. At the first one I tried to see—an old *buron* that had been turned into a museum—I found the gate posted with a sign reading, "MALADIE CONTAGIEUSE, Défense de Pénétrer, ACCÈS INTERDIT" and a letter explaining that the premises had been placed under surveillance because of *charbon bactéridien.* At another *buron* museum—one happily not infected by anthrax—I was reprimanded for taking pictures, and the guide whipped a crowd of French retirees into low, menacing rumbles just by mentioning raw milk and American pressure on European markets in the same breath. After the group broke up he admonished me yet again, this time for recording his presentation. I left in something of a hurry.

Then, at one farm I visited I happened to mention that I intended to travel to Salers and that I was interested in the local cheese. The farmer responded, "Oh, down that way there's an exceptional cheesemaker to see. He makes his *fromage* in a *buron* in the old way." When I asked where, he pulled out his cell phone to call a friend who knew. "He still milks his cows by hand," he told me while we waited for the call to go through. "It's authentic." Though I would later figure out that this was the Taillé *buron,* the friend didn't know when exactly I could visit. The farmer promised to call me later with more details, but I never heard from him. I made more inquiries and scoured brochures for addresses, with little luck. Finally, I contacted Hervé Mons, who instantly said he would be more than happy to take me to the *buron,* except he had to go to Japan to talk with some cheese buyers there. When I called again during my next stay in France, the Japanese buyers were visiting him, and he couldn't go then, either. I started to get the feeling he wasn't too keen on journalists, especially when he told me, "I don't trust journalists."

In the end, I found Guy Chambon's *buron* listed in the back of a little book about Salers that I'd bought, skimmed, and then tossed into the back of a French rental car some months earlier. "*Une superbe adresse,*" the book gushed. No matter the glowing recommendation, however, the Chambons themselves didn't seem particularly eager for visitors. When I called, Guy's wife, Marie-Jo, answered and said, "Yeah, yeah, come whenever; just call the day before," before abruptly hanging up. As I put down my phone, I wondered what exactly it was about hand-milking that so attracted me. And yet I knew. There was something in the thought of seeing raw milk come straight from the cows, with no machines to intercede, no mechanical slurping, nothing but human and beast. I wanted to be there in the predawn chill as the cheesemakers milked. I wanted to watch guys balance on one-legged stools amid the sound of cowbells, see the milk froth in their buckets. I wanted to see *le top.*

THE CHAMBONS' PLACE, snugged into the bottom of a rise as smooth as a tablecloth, was surrounded by a fence of wire and wooden posts nearly falling in on itself. The moon hung to one side of the barely brightened sky, and in the pale light I could make out a two-door car and a gray truck parked next to a rusted livestock trailer at the end of the ragged, red-dirt drive. The *buron* itself had a sturdy air, and as the light went up, it looked rather like a speckled egg, with gray and rust and beige field-stones suspended in newish mortar. A fringe of bushes sprouted along one wall.

Two dimly lit people were sending calves across the muddy track toward another dim form who stood amid a herd of cows. One of the two was Julien, a sweet-faced twentysomething with a shock of tousled brown hair—the summer help. The other was Marie-Jo, a slight figure with pixie-cut hair, wearing a sweater and blue jeans. I asked after M. Chambon. "He's up there," Julien said, waving at the other side of the rise.

I called a greeting to Marie-Jo, who didn't seem to hear. I could well imagine that she found the continual visits by tourists wearing. Things would have been quieter back when many *burons* weren't accessible by roads that any pesky cheese-loving sightseer could easily navigate. One can only imagine how she might have felt to have been part-owner of a *buron* in the thick of what was known as the "whey cure." At the turn of the twentieth century, during *la belle époque,* a health official claimed that whey could stimulate the liver and kidneys and help eliminate toxins from the body. Soon thereafter, a number of *buron* makers found themselves invaded each morning by men dressed nattily in suits and vests and women toting parasols, all arriving to take their cup of elixir before setting off on a morning constitutional in the mountains.

But making small talk while we chased animals at the crack of dawn didn't seem like a great idea anyway, and so I trailed along silently in the dewy path blazed through the grass by the calves. We reached the spot where Guy stood surrounded by the low-slung backs of cows. They were kept together for milking by a wire strung along pickets, which I discovered was electrified when I bumped against it. Marie-Jo helped Julien corral the babies into a makeshift wooden pen. Safely enclosed and still awkward with youth, the calves jostled against one another, some sticking their heads between the slats to peer out at us and their mothers. Marie-Jo pulled up one of the pickets to allow me into the enclosure with Guy and the cows. "He's over there," she said, gesturing. "Ask him anything you want."

"Bonjour," I said, walking over.

He nodded my way, *"Bonjour."*

Guy was a big man, a fact made plainer by the royal blue Carhartt-type jumpsuit he wore. When he stood outlined alongside the reddish flank of one of his cows, the blue crescent of his belly rounded before him like a soup bowl. He appeared to be fiftyish, and had wispy, thinning hair that made him look a little like the Gerber baby, only with more wrinkles. When he laughed, it was one of those wheezing laughs that sounds like a half-sneeze. And as the morning went on, it became clear that Guy liked to laugh. When he saw me snapping pictures of Julien, for instance, he called out, "You can take him home with you!" When I protested that I was just trying to document the milking, he said, "No, no, I mean you can take home the *picture*." He reminded me of the type of guy my dad, who worked as a foreman in a canning plant, might have thrown back brewskies with at the local tavern.

Guy was not, that is, very much like the sort of person you might imagine would insist upon making traditional cheese. In the States, the neo-hippie, neo-agrarian movement has made it rather fashionable to quit a high-paying job in the city, buy some herd animals, and start making *fromage*. Then, of course, you're supposed to write a book about how going back to the land and making cheese has changed you by putting you back in touch with an ancient rhythm of life. There's nothing wrong with this movement, and it has produced some pretty good books, too. But in France, people tend to make cheese because, well, they're cheesemakers. When I asked Guy why he made cheese in the old way, with all Salers cows, he shrugged and said, "*C'est comme ça*"—"That's how it is."

This doesn't mean he was without philosophy. As I watched him work that morning, he would sometimes stare fixedly at what he was doing, as if he'd forgotten I was there. Then he would think of something he wanted to tell me and stop to say, "You're all rich in America," or "You know America is an imperial power," or "You have bad agriculture in America." He told me he'd seen a show about the United States on television one evening where they'd been talking about how to reeducate Americans to eat better. "You need *des écoles du goût,*" he said. "What?" I said. "Tasting schools," he said. "You need schools where people can learn how to taste." People in America eat too much, he explained. Then he added, "Of course, they do in France, too," wheezing happily and grabbing at his stomach.

Few things can compare to being lectured on a mountainside on how to eat well by a Frenchman who probably outweighs you by a good hundred pounds. But the French generally tend to believe that taste—which is what leads to proper eating, of course—is an absolute: a conclusion to be reached through careful study of the sample at hand. In French, the verb for "to taste" is *goûter.* The noun for "a tasting," however, comes from the verb *déguster,* which means "to savor." For the French, savoring cheese, at least in theory, is like performing scientific classification, a task to which one applies method and precision. The French continue to believe this in spite of decades of research showing that taste perception can differ significantly from person to person. This is not merely theory—our tongues are actually laden with varying concentrations of little toadstool-shaped taste receptors known as fungiform papillae. A lot of tasting also makes use of our noses, compounding the problem: studies have shown that the nose is the most suggestible of organs. For instance, when given hits of butyric acid to sniff and told it's a food scent, people will say it smells like parmesan cheese; if they're told it's a body scent, they're more likely to say it smells like armpits or vomit.

No matter what the French say about the art of tasting, they don't often appear to go very deep themselves. Maybe I simply wasn't in the right places, or maybe it was because I was an American and they didn't want to intimidate me, but I didn't see a whole lot of meticulous savoring while I traveled around the country looking for cheese. Even in *The Assassinated Cheeses,* Légasse, a food writer, rarely describes the taste of the various cheeses he and his companions are sampling. When he does, his most extensive comments amount to "persistent, floral, milky and at the same time unctuous and round." And when Guy and I later shared slices of one of his aged Salers, he tilted his head and said simply, *"C'est piquant"*—"It's sharp."

IN ANY CASE, as the dawn unfolded, there wasn't a whole lot of time for disquisitions. It was time, instead, for milking. Guy and his two helpers set about their task directly. Whether by hand or by machine, milking is an unrelenting business. Lactating animals must be milked seven days a week, no exceptions, no vacations, twice a day, without fail. And if you own a herd of all Salers cows, part of what you get to do twice a day, without fail, is wrestle calves. This is where the nutcase part comes in, and why producers of Salers cheeses who use only this breed get to stamp the words "Tradition Salers" on the ends of their *fourmes.* (This in addition to the usual "Salers, Salers" that gets stamped on all Salers cheeses.) Few people would know better than Guy what it takes to earn that distinction. He was five when his parents bought the *buron* in 1960, and ten when he milked his first cow. "You can start that early?" I asked, startled.

"Yes," he said, looking suddenly earnest, "when you have love."

Love is a big word, but watching them, I had to admit that it's about the only one to explain why anyone would keep and milk Salers cows. The milking went something like this: Marie-Jo and Julien would walk to the calf pen and scream, "*Allez!*" Then they'd yell out the names of the mother cows, because the calves didn't yet have names of their own. (So if I had been milking Lulabelle, I would have had to stand in front of the pen and scream, "Lulabelle!") And then the calf would come, sort of, if it felt like it, balking, its head hung low. After the calf had been extracted from the pen, it had to be muscled to the correct mother. Finally at its mother's side, each calf clamped its lips to a salmon-colored teat for a moment or two, getting the milk going, and then there was another scuffle to pull the now eagerly feeding calf from the udders and get it looped to its mother's flank with a short length of rope. As the cow was milked the calf stood with its neck tied to its mother, drooling milky saliva and wearing an absurd look of satiety. Once the mother was milked out, the calf was released, whereupon it would nudge the empty teats, licking and pulling as it looked for the dregs. And then the process started all over again.

As I watched, the sun rose, turning the cows and their calves penny-red—local lore says they're that color because they were "licked by lava." I walked through the warming air to the other side of the rise, cowbells chiming all around. There I stood looking back at the herd and the humans tending it, three figures moving in a cluster of russet. Beyond them was only the green arc of the horizon and a sky streaked with cobalt-tinted cirrus. It was a glorious morning for a milking, and I was there. I'd arrived at *le top*.

It wasn't quite the top I'd imagined, however. Even from a distance, Guy's red-and-white circa 1968 International 523 tractor was unmistakable at the center of the herd. It was ramshackle and mud-caked and missing a headlight, but beneath it, a pipe rotated busily, generating power for the portable *machines à traire* that Guy, Marie-Jo, and Julien were industriously attaching to one set of udders after another. They had a few moments of respite as the machines pumped—at one point, Marie-Jo perched on the lid of one machine and yawned—and then they sprang back into motion. The machines were simple affairs, just a cluster of sleeves that slipped over the teats and attached to a tall metal milk jug, but they were indisputably machines. Not so much as a single one-legged milking stool was in sight. "How long have you been using those?" I'd asked Guy. He paused to consider. He thought they'd got them in 2003.

Truth be told, I'd had a bad feeling, even though the weathered Buron d'Algour sign at the top of the road to their place had held out the faded promise: "*Traite à la main.*" Not long before my visit, I had gotten hold of a book, *Sentinelles des montagnes,* which appeared in 2008 and documents the history of *estives* in central France with photographs of crumbling, long-deserted *burons*. The section of the book about the few remaining active places featured pictures of Mons's *buron* cheesemaker. There were also images of the Chambons that very clearly showed a system of thick rubber tubes that I'd not wanted to truly believe belonged to the milking machines attached to the cows. But of course they did. Of course.

"So you don't milk by hand anymore at all?" I said to Guy, even though the reply was obvious.

"No."

TAKING THE ROAD out of Auvergne the next day, I stopped by the Puy Mary—the most emblematic of the peaks near Salers, part of the serrated remnants of what was once the largest stratovolcano in Europe. I parked behind a row of cars at a snack stand near the summit and then climbed the steep, winding footpaths to the top. The ridges looked like massive, rocky vertebrae twisting off into more peaks beyond; I thought I could discern the telltale circular scars left over from prehistoric explosions. Scrims of low-hanging clouds shifted on the horizon, and nearby, an iron cross leaned crookedly over a pile of rocks. I stayed awhile, until the chiding of the wind persuaded me to return to my car.

Back at home, I watched *The Assassinated Cheeses* on DVD

and brooded. Not to have seen one of the most iconic acts in all of French cheesemaking—it seemed a terrible loss. Meanwhile, there on my screen was Hervé Mons watching Marcel Taillé with his little one-legged stool strapped to his backside; there was Périco Légasse—drat the man—with his acolyte Svensson in tow. I watched it once. I watched it a second time. And then I noticed something strange.

If you were a regular French person who didn't know a whole lot about cows and milking and who had never seen a portable milking machine, and if you were watching television half-asleep on your living room couch after dinner, the way most French people would watch—nothing interesting comes on French TV until late in the evening because before that, of course, everyone is at table, dining—you would likely see something like this: a brief shot of Taillé walking away from the camera and toward a cow while two of his helpers tend cows nearby, then a shot of Mons saying, "Let me introduce you," and then a shot of one of the helpers squatted beneath a pair of russet flanks and milking into a pail. The camera pans back to where Taillé stands in front of the first cow, which the other helper is also milking by hand. Then the men walk forward and begin exchanging *Bonjours*.

But if you were, say, a person who knew what portable milking machines looked like and were watching carefully, stopping and rewinding, and really looking, you would see this: a brief shot of Taillé walking toward a cow while his two helpers stand near cows with suction cups attached to their udders, then a shot of Mons saying, "Let me introduce you." And then the camera panning back over a scene in which the milking machines have magically popped out of existence.

The entire hand-milking was staged. There is no other explanation. To get the shots as they appear in the film, the film crew would have had to stop their cameras and wait as the machines were stowed and the milking stools and pails fetched. They would have had to wait as the men settled into place, crouching at the flanks of cows they'd been milking moments before by machine. They would have had to wait, that is, as the players took their places. The aesthetic reasons for wanting to film a hand-milking are easy to understand—it makes for a much prettier picture—but the way the editors put the scene together is questionable. It might be argued that this *traite à la main* was done for demonstration purposes, but there's no indication of that in the film. The viewer is left to assume that this is how things are still done. That everything here is exactly as it's always been.

The whole thing put me in mind of something I once saw at the Salon International de l'Agriculture, a huge national agricultural fair held annually on the outskirts of Paris. In one corner, near the livestock pens, was an automatic voluntary milking system, or VMS, made by the Swedish firm DeLaval, which features a large, robotic milking stanchion into which the cow walks whenever the urge strikes. According to the promotional materials, the many benefits of the machines include a hydraulic robotic arm equipped with teat cleaners for "optimum teat sanitation"; two lasers and an image-processing system for "precise, quick teat detection"; ultra-clean suction cups that attach to the udders for milking; "four optical auto-milk meters" that instantly divert any "abnormal" milk; and "automatic teat disinfection" afterward. Detailed readouts on milk yield and quality are displayed on the onboard computer screen. Next to the VMS stood a companion machine, the "world-acclaimed DeLaval swinging cow brush," a huge, bristly yellow roller of the sort you see in a car wash, ruthlessly poised to clean the flank of a life-size model of a cow painted with the blue, white, and red stripes of *liberté, égalité* and *fraternité*. It was all a far cry from the pastoral ideal that typically comes to mind when we think of dairying in the French countryside.

Of course, a few small portable milking machines are not a VMS. And you still get raw milk with a milking machine. But the trouble is, wherever there is technology, science is never far behind—and the two together pose a distinct threat, at least according to the traditional French way of thinking. People such as Légasse see the hypersanitization of the cow as part of an ever-increasing hypersanitization of milk, all part of an insidious impulse to "sterilize everything." Even raw milk is now ultra-clean, "too clean," more than one cheesemaker would tell me. Though the French are predictably happy to blame one another—Pasteur was, after all, undeniably French—there is also a lingering suspicion that much of this alarming emphasis on cleanliness migrated to their shores from across the Atlantic. Just take a look at American grocery stores, with their complimentary antibacterial wipes and ubiquitous bottles of hand sanitizer. Nor have the French forgotten the U.S. FDA's efforts in the early 2000s to get the World Health Organization to institute a ban on raw-milk cheeses—not only in the United States, but also in all member countries worldwide. Had it been approved, the measure would have wrested *fromages au lait cru* from the French on their own soil.

So portable milking machines in a *buron* are not merely unlovely: they symbolize the creeping menace of mechanized, American-style sanitation. Any sort of technology, any hint of science, is problematic. Even if most French people realize that most cheese today is not made on a mountaintop out of milk that has been gathered by hand, the idea that some cheese, somewhere, is made this way is important. The untainted cheese must endure.

Because if *le top* of French cheesemaking has been compromised, the consequences could be drastic, indeed. The final scene of *The Assassinated Cheeses* features Légasse speaking with another well-known *affineur,* a man named Philippe Olivier. "If the unfortunate day should arrive when we have almost no more *fromages au lait cru,*" Olivier says, "all of the other cheeses will also disappear."

"The industrialized cheeses will disappear?" Légasse says.

"Yes, they'll sell fewer and fewer of them. Because what makes the image of our country?" He looks upward and gestures toward the sky, as if imploring the Almighty, voice quickening and rising with fervor as he answers his own question: "It's the cheeses. It's the real, historic cheeses that have made our culture. It's those sorts of cheeses, and not these cheeses that are produced one after the other like caramels. That's not it, that's not it," he exclaims, head wagging like a schoolmarm's. "That's not cheese!"

Lose raw-milk cheeses, that is, and you lose the whole *fromage*.

THE DILEMMA OF MILK

~~~~~~~~~~~~~

"A corpse is meat gone bad. Well and what's cheese?
Corpse of milk."

—JAMES JOYCE

I once tried to make cheese using sour cream and a pair of nylons. My belief in the possible success of this method may seem questionable, and yet it's true that the basic cheesemaking process is simple. Take some milk, curdle it, drain off the liquid whey, dump the curds in a mold, *et voilà*: cheese! I'd found the sour-cream-and-nylons technique in a book, where it appeared under the words "A Simple Cheese: A recipe you can make at home that uses nylon stockings." Granted, the nylon stocking part did give me pause, but mostly I found myself intrigued. After all, what better way to begin comprehending the French passion for cheese than to make some with what could be considered lingerie? The book also claimed that the recipe was derived from a soft farmhouse cheese from Wiltshire, England, thereby tempering the raciness with a reassuring, British air. So I went out and bought some sour cream (the book's suggested replacement for the raw cream from Wiltshire originally used to make the cheese) and some knee-high stockings.

The package containing my nylons sat on the kitchen counter for several days, bizarrely out of place next to bread crumbs, the seedy remains of chopped tomatoes, a cup half-filled with cold coffee. Finally, one morning, I unwrapped them: light taupe stretch sheers with a reinforced top. The choice of stocking color had caused a mild predicament. If I chose "suntan," would I get a different cheese from what I'd get if I used "nude"? What if I used black stockings? Would I end up with gray cheese? And what about the chemicals in those dyes? Was I about to make a sexy, English-style, carcinogen-laced soft farmhouse cheese? Taupe had seemed a middle ground. The recipe said to place one stocking inside the other. Then "put them in a 1-quart plastic container and stretch the elastic edge over the top, forming a well." I grabbed a plastic bowl that looked about right and stretched the reinforced top around the rim. The resulting well brought to mind the word *orifice*. I spooned a pint of sour cream into the well, where it settled downward into a good-size lump at the toe.

I next tugged the stocking free from the lip of the bowl in

preparation for a series of instructions that read, "Wrap the elastic end of the stocking round the neck of a quart bottle that is full. Place the bottle on the shelf of a refrigerator, allowing the stocking full of cream to hang down in front of the shelf." I opened the fridge and cast a speculative glance at its contents. To what does one tie one's sour-cream-filled stocking in the inexplicable absence of a one-quart bottle that is full? Could I somehow lasso it to a carton of milk? Doubtful. Same for the bottle of Napoleon capers and the Pace Chunky Salsa. I eyed a half-empty flask of gin, but in the end settled on a bottle of unopened champagne extracted from a nearby cubbyhole, knotting the long, stretchy calf of the nylon around its neck. After much rearranging of leftovers, the cream-filled toe dangled from one of my refrigerator shelves, the "delicious whey" promised by the recipe already draining neatly into the container I'd placed below.

Over the next few days, I opened the door every so often to peer at the stocking suspended from the shelf, where it looked rather like an upside-down exclamation point. My partner, Chris, who had been out of town when I began my experiment, went in search of a snack not long after his return. "Why is there champagne in the fridge?" he wanted to know.

I said, "You didn't really look, did you?"

He looked again. "What the . . . ?" and then, "Oh, are you making cheese?" I said I was. "I thought maybe it was a giant testicle," he said. "I leave for a week and a half and you have giant men's testicles in there . . ."

I'd begun the cheese experiment on a Monday; the following

Sunday, I took out the nylon. The entire top had dried solid, and I cut through the stocking to get at the "cheese." Earlier in the day I'd guessed it would taste like refrigerator. Chris said, "I bet it will taste like stocking." Given that Chris is a man who believes raw chicken is a hazardous material in need of near-industrial-grade safety measures, I decided not to mention the possible chemical dye–cancer connection. The desiccated top cracked off as I peeled back the fabric. I cut a thin slice from the drier end. "Hmm," I said. "Tastes like goat cheese."

"Let me taste," Chris said, then, "Yep, it does taste like goat cheese." The softer, rounded end tasted sort of like cream cheese. But mostly the entire thing tasted like solidified sour cream. Six days and a pair of perfectly good nylons, and I'd managed to create vertical sour cream. Amusing as it was to work with nylons and dairy products in my refrigerator, it seemed this method wasn't going to yield the information I needed.

Because what I really wanted to understand was the power and mystique of traditional French cheese—what made it so compelling that a bunch of adult Frenchmen would fake a hand-milking just to keep that mystique alive? In spite of the obvious hyperbole of Philippe Olivier's claim that all French cheeses would disappear if raw-milk cheeses disappeared—what a sight it would be to walk into, say, an American supermarket and watch all the pucks of Babybel instantly dematerialize—his words roused my curiosity. What exactly was it about cheese that led to such fervor?

If my cheese experiment had shown me one thing, it was the

depth of my ignorance. I may have grown up loving cheese, but I realized anew that I didn't know all that much about it. Where had cheese even come from in the first place? I needed to find out more about cheese in general—its science, its art, its place in human history—and French cheese in particular. I needed to go back to the beginning.

THAT BEGINNING, it turns out, is rather murky: no one can really say for sure how cheese began. According to an oft-told legend, some long-forgotten inhabitant of Mesopotamia took off on a journey one day with fresh milk safely stowed in a lamb's stomach, the prehistoric equivalent of a Ziploc baggie. At lunchtime he opened it to find that the liquid had somehow transformed into chunky, edible white stuff in just a matter of hours. Milk's natural acidity will cause it to curdle—i.e., spoil—all on its own. You've seen this phenomenon in your refrigerator if you've ever left a carton of milk too long and had to pour out the gloppy chunks. But the nomad with the lamb's stomach had discovered that this spoiling could be quickened and controlled with whatever was in that stomach; he had stumbled upon the rudiments of making one of the world's oldest convenience foods. Today we take for granted our ability to turn liquid milk into solid cheese. To the guy from Mesopotamia, however, few things could have been more incredible—or more valuable.

What to do with excess milk had been a common problem

almost as soon as people began herding animals, starting with sheep in modern-day Iran and Iraq around 9,000–7,000 BCE. Sheep were the first ruminants to be tamed (and the second domesticated animal overall, after the dog), followed soon thereafter by goats. Cows—the animal we most often associate with cheese today—meandered into the picture a thousand or so years later. Though sheep, goats, and cows are the most familiar dairying animals, cheese is so handy that people make it with the milk of all sorts of creatures. These include horses, water buffalo, and reindeer—in Lapland people dunk the cheese made from reindeer milk in coffee as if it were toast. Meanwhile, in Switzerland, the world's most expensive cheese is made with the milk of moose. According to one article, moose give very little milk and are so temperamental that they go dry if milked in anything but absolute silence. The resulting delicacy retails for $420 per pound.

In our society we have such easy access to so many foods that it can be hard to recall how crucial milk has been throughout human history. That milk is key to the creation of cheese would seem obvious, but it bears repeating in an age in which most of us trace the origins of our cheese back to the supermarket cooler and no farther. Even I, with my dairy-filled family history, can find this fact easy to overlook. Yet the story of cheese is really the story of milk. Cheese is milk made solid, preservable, portable. Cheese is milk that gets around.

As food expert Harold McGee reminds us, the very word

mammal means "creature of the breast," and human mothers' milk is what allows our brains to keep developing during infancy. When we eat cheese, we're essentially consuming breast milk, an idea that some people today find rather strange—or worse. Take for example the sassy authors of the popular diet guide *Skinny Bitch,* who begin a chapter entitled "The Dairy Disaster" as follows: "Go suck your mother's tits. Go on. Suck your mother's tits. You think this is ridiculous? It is." This ridiculousness is compounded, they argue, when we consume the breast milk of a different species. Not only are dairy products disgusting for adults, the authors contend, but they're unhealthy and will turn you into a grossly fat, pimply creature who (the inference is clear) cannot get a date. We believe they're good for us, they claim, only because the dairy industry's multibillion-dollar marketing campaigns have convinced us it's so: "Milk does a body good!"

Let us pause for a moment, however, and consider the cow. If human mothers are good at producing nourishment for their children, they're nothing next to nonhuman ones. In one study conducted by the University of Florida, researchers found that in ten months, "a good cow can produce 496 pounds of protein, 784 pounds of energy in the form of sugar lactose, 560 pounds of fat and 112 pounds of minerals all in 16,000 pounds of milk." That's enough protein, they state, to keep one man going for ten years, enough energy for five years, and enough calcium for thirty. Though the type of cow used for the study was no doubt a robust, modern breed, even in ancient times a good cow could mean the difference between life and death for an entire family, and still does in some parts of the world.

If early humans spent time ruminating the role of the ruminants in their lives, no doubt it was to wonder just how grazing animals managed the trick of turning grasses and flowers and other forbs into milk at all. It is not an easy process. For starters, cows don't even have teeth—or at least not upper incisors. Instead, they have a hard "dental pad" on the top front of their mouths. Using this in conjunction with their bottom incisors, they tear up some 110 pounds of greenery daily, spending six to eight hours a day just chewing. As they chew, they swish the stems and petals and blades of grass around with their tongues, forming roundish masses of chewed food called boluses. These boluses then pass from a cow's mouth into its stomach for digestion. This sounds straightforward, but a ruminant stomach is an advanced and complicated piece of biological machinery.

Where we have just one stomach, ruminants have four—or, rather, one stomach with four distinct chambers. Perhaps one of the best ways to appreciate the strangeness of this is by watching an episode of *The French Chef* with Julia Child entitled "Tripes à la mode." Nothing quite surpasses the image of Julia with an entire cow's stomach—the stomach of a ruminant makes up a fifth of its body weight—that she's had express-delivered from New Hampshire in order to make tripe. "Nowadays you find a lot of people who don't even know what tripe is!" she trills with a gay though slightly bemused air, as though she can't quite imagine how this alarming gap in knowledge has come to pass. (How her heart would have been gladdened to know about offal's recent comeback in gourmet circles.) Tripe, she explains, is made with the walls of the various stomach chambers; it is French "soul food." She points to a diagram showing each chamber, beginning with the first and largest, the rumen, which has a capacity of some twenty-five gallons. Next is the reticulum, lined with intricate netlike folds of tissue. It's called the "honeycomb," Child tells the audience, as she picks up the enormous, fleshy bag and flops it about until she finds the chamber. "Looks almost like a face," she says, though unless she's talking about the face of a *Star Trek* alien, the resemblance is difficult to spot.

In a living cow, half-digested goo swishes between the reticulum and rumen every minute or so, with boluses brought back up to the cow's mouth so she can break down and soften the cud even more. Each day, cows make fifteen to twenty gallons of saliva (enough to fill the average bathtub), to neutralize the acidity of the fermenting cud so that the billions of bacteria in the rumen can operate. That's a lot of drool. To gauge how well that drool, and the digestion process generally, is working, researchers will sometimes cut a hole through a cow's side into the rumen. These "cannulated cows," or "cows with a window," go on as though there's nothing out of the ordinary. In fact, they barely notice when people walk up and stick their hands and whole arms into the rumen—one schoolkid who tried it reported that the stuff

inside felt like a squishy mixture of warm grass and peanut butter. Farther down, he said, it was like a melting Wendy's Frosty.

Plant fibers are so tough to digest that they can stay in the first
two chambers for as long as two days before passing to the oma-
sum, or "book" stomach, lined with pagelike folds that absorb
fatty acids and other nutrients. Then, finally, there's the "true"
stomach, the abomasum, the one that functions much like our
own. And when all this is done, of course, we humans come
along and steal the milk.

THOSE WHO SAY it's unhealthy to consume the milk of other
species sometimes point out that cheese—especially the simple,
unaged cheese that most ancient peoples would have eaten—
presents something of a challenge to the human digestive system.
Lactose, one of the milk sugars found in cheese, must be broken
down before the human body can absorb it. In aged cheeses, helpful lactase bacteria do this job during the aging process. In order
to digest younger cheeses, however, people must produce their
own lactase enzymes, an ability that declines after childhood
for much of the world's population. But several thousand years
ago, people in certain parts of the globe developed the ability to
keep on producing lactase well into adulthood, a useful trait that
spread throughout those populations—and a good indication of
how helpful cheese can be to human survival. In other words,
those of us who can eat cheese and remain blissfully flatulence-

free—a group that includes 98 percent of Scandinavians, 90 percent of French and Germans, 40 percent of southern Europeans and North Africans, and 30 percent of African Americans—are genetic mutants. Very fortunate genetic mutants.

Even before the mutation (and presumably with a fair amount of gastrointestinal distress), cheesemaking was so important that it spread far and wide over large portions of the ancient world. In the Sahara, 7,000-year-old cave art is thought to depict cheesemaking, while Neolithic-era ceramic pots with holes for draining curd have been found at archaeological sites in Burgundy and the French Jura. The upper panel of a 4,500-year-old mosaic from Mesopotamia depicts a line of cows, while in the lower panel, skirted men set about milking and making butter and cheese. People also milk and curdle in Sumerian bas-reliefs from 3,500 BCE, while cylindrical jars squirreled away in tombs in Abydos hold traces of real cheese dating to Egypt's first dynastic period, no doubt placed there to give the desert kings something to nibble in the afterlife. The Greeks were evidently fond of shaving slivers of hardened cheese into their beverages: In Homer's *Iliad,* a slave prepares a mixture of grated *chèvre* and wine, and in the *Odyssey,* Circe uses a similar concoction of wine, cheese, and honey to drug Odysseus and his men. Nearly every cheese history ever written further notes that later in the tale, the Cyclops makes cheese using wicker baskets called *formos*—possibly the origin of the word *fromage.*

By the time of the Romans, a judiciously chosen cheese could heal, keep you forever young, help conquer countries, or even kill. Pliny the Elder, in his *Naturalis historiae,* contends that new, unsalted cheese is easiest on the stomach, warns that "old [i.e., aged] cheese has a binding effect on the bowels," and recommends "fresh cheese, applied with honey" to "effac[e] the marks of bruises." His most extraordinary claim, however, is that "Zoroaster lived thirty years in the wilderness on cheese, prepared in such a peculiar manner, that he was insensible to the advances of old age." Cheese, the fountain of youth! The reputed revitalizing powers of cheese might explain why Roman legionnaires received twenty-seven grams of it as part of their standard rations (along with grain, meat, lard, salt, and wine) under the emperor Hadrian. Be that as it may, however, too much cheese could have quite the opposite effect: Hadrian's successor, Antonius Pius, is said to have died in 161 CE after overindulging his taste for Banon, a chestnut-leaf wrapped goat cheese from Provence.

Most of the cheeses in ancient times would have been relatively rudimentary. Though ancient peoples knew that combining milk with pieces of the stomach of a young ruminant—what we call rennet—worked to coagulate the liquid, they didn't really know how this worked. They thought cheesemaking was sort of like baby-making, and that maybe the rennet mixed with the milk to create cheese in the same way that semen mixed with fluids in the female body. In reality, rennet contains an enzyme called chymosin that helps casein, a protein in milk, clump into a solid mass by clipping off parts of the protein molecule that normally repel one another. The remaining dozen or so milk proteins then swirl around the solid caseins in liquid suspension. The result is what Little Miss Muffet would have called curds and whey.

The French name for curds and whey is *fromage frais*—"fresh cheese." In France you can often find it for sale in special perforated cheese molds called *faisselles*. These are layered into a larger container so that the whey keeps the curd wet. Sometimes the curds might be drained or molded a bit, but *fromage frais* is still essentially just unprocessed curd—smooth and white, with a texture and taste rather like that of plain yogurt. It's incredibly basic and rustic—one variety from Provence is even called *brousse,* meaning "brush," or "scrubland." (If you're *en pleine brousse,* you're "out in the sticks.") Few things make me happier than going to a French village market, spotting a little whey-filled tub with a circle of moist, bald curd bobbing in its center, and knowing that breakfast the next morning will be *fromage frais* and strawberries sprinkled with a spoonful of raw sugar.

Fromage frais makes such a good foil for things such as fruit because curds are so bland, the blank slate onto which all other cheeses are writ. As time went on, people realized that not only could curds preserve fresh milk, but if you manipulated them the right way, they could taste even better and be far more interesting. Perhaps one of the most amazing things about cheese is that something as blah as cheese curds can be turned into a dazzling array of hundreds and even thousands of cheeses.

Of course, that array can seem more daunting than dazzling if the cheeses are French, and you're an American who grew up under the impression that the most remarkable *fromage* ever invented was Cheez Whiz. Nevertheless, even the strangest of French cheeses falls into one of two broad, self-explanatory types: *frais* or *sec*—"fresh" or "dry." Through the mid-1800s, in fact, these were essentially the only two categories of cheese in France.

Though we might rejoice at the ease of such a system, having just two big categories seemed rather limiting to a student of Pasteur's, one Émile Duclaux. Considered the founder of dairy microbiology, in the 1870s Duclaux conducted extensive experiments on the process of fermenting cheese. Eventually he devised a system for classifying cheeses based on how they were made, a typology that has survived virtually unchanged. In this schema, "fresh" cheeses became soft cheeses, or *pâtes molles* (*pâte* being what's inside the rind and *molle* meaning "soft"). Soft cheeses are further classified by their rinds—*la croûte*. The rind is either "washed" with various bacteria-encouraging liquids, to create a *croûte lavée,* or "flowered" with various molds, which results in a *croûte fleurie.* The "dry" cheeses became hard cheeses, or *pâtes dures.* To remove the moisture from these cheeses, makers either press the curd to make a *pâte pressée,* or press and "cook" the curd for a *pâte pressée cuite.* Finally, there are blue cheeses, *les fromages bleus,* which have been infected with various strains of penicillium. These are also sometimes called *à pâte persillée*—

"parsley-ed"—because the mold looks like parsley sprinkled through the cheese. All in all, that makes for only five basic *fromage* types, or one for each finger.

BUT IF THERE are only a handful of basic types, how, then, did the French come to create so many hundreds of varieties? The answer to that query begins, as it must, with God.

Where the Almighty goes in France, so too goes cheese. This became particularly true after the fall of the Roman Empire. As the Dark Ages spread across Europe, monasteries became sanctums of cheese knowledge, helping to keep cheesemaking technology alive. This pairing of God and *fromage* must have made a sort of intuitive sense, historically speaking. There's reason to believe people worshipped cows in prehistoric times; images of aurouchs, the wild ancestors of cows, decorate the walls at Lascaux and other archaeological sites in southwestern France. Milk and butter appear in many Indo-European creation stories (the Hittites even placated weather gods with cheese), and in the Old Testament. The Bible, in fact, positively overflows with dairy goodness—you can scarcely turn the page without running across a reference to butter or curds or milk and honey.

What's more, cheesemaking was a natural fit with monastic life. One of the best places in France to see this still is the Abbaye de Tamié, a complex of pale stone buildings tucked below a peak in the French Alps. Founded in 1132, Tamié is home to an order of Trappist monks for whom the quiet, contemplative labor of cheesemaking is a means of arriving at a deeper understanding of God. Signboards in the abbey's small grass-roofed shop show monks reverently examining the round disks of Tamié cheese that they age in their vaulted *caves*. Each bears a white label dotted with a blue *cross formée*—a twelfth- and thirteenth-century forerunner to the Maltese cross, each of its eight points symbolizing virtues such as faith, humility, and wholeheartedness.

From the shop, a long driveway passes between Alpine flowers and a high, moss-furred stone wall. Partway down this lane lies the doorway to a seventeenth-century church where the monks gather to chant *les offices* seven times a day. I arrived one day near *sexte,* the office of the sixth hour after dawn—i.e., noon. It's an auspicious hour for prayer, the hour when the sun is full, the Divine at its splendorous pinnacle. Sitting in the pews felt hushed and worshipful, with the only light coming from windows set high above an altar at one end of the nave. A white-haired monk knelt motionless on the stone floor, waiting. As the time for the chant drew close, more monks appeared in ones and twos, eighteen in all, some old and knotty-limbed, some young. Most are involved in one way or another with the *fromagerie*. Bells rang out above. I thought of cows. We stood and, to my surprise, everyone sang, including the parishioners who had filled the seats around me. A green photocopy of the music found its way into my hands, and I joined in—badly, judging from the oblique glances of the Frenchwoman beside me. The *caves* for Tamié are located below the cloisters, and the monks like to joke that the notes sink down to imbue the cheeses as they age. I could only hope my contribution hadn't spoiled a good batch.

After the last sounds died away, the bells pealed again. Outside the church a faint path led up and away into the trees. I followed it until I could look down into the walled abbey, the tidy buildings surrounded by grass so green it nearly seemed to vibrate. Here and there, European larches broke the top of the wall, silhouetted against the ridgelines beyond. Larches can grow to be over a hundred feet tall and live for six hundred years: those at the abbey must have witnessed the birth of thousands of cheeses over the centuries. Standing there, it was easy to imagine how a cheese made in such a place might inspire feelings of reverence. To a medieval peasant, eating such a *fromage* must have felt like an almost holy act.

AND YET, WHEN most people today think of monastery-style cheeses—there are so many that some French experts put them in their own category—reverence is probably not the first word that leaps to mind. The most salient feature of rind-washed cheeses (the sort usually made by monks) is that they stink. The French writer Zola described one such cheese with an odor so strong that it made flies swoon about the serving platter, so that they "lay fallen about the round on the grey-veined marble." Blessed food or no, these cheeses must have tested the devotion of even the most worshipful peasant. Among the stinkiest is Époisses de Bourgogne—so smelly I once read it was banned on French public transportation. (When I asked an Époisses maker about the supposed ban, she said carrying an Époisses onto a bus wasn't illegal, just not recommended. Meanwhile, the odor of her nearby cheeses manifested itself as an almost corporeal presence.) Époisses is thought to have been invented at the Abbaye de Fontenay, where it reportedly did test the devotion of followers in a very real way: the monks are said to have employed it in trials by ordeal. "Was it supposed," muses Patrick Rance, "that only the guilty could not stomach its honest power?" It's unclear from the stories how exactly the cheese was used to threaten the accused, but one does wonder just how much Époisses would need to be consumed to prove one's innocence.

The reason for all of this smelliness is something known as *Brevibacterium linens*—which happen to be the same sort of bacteria that grow on human skin and make your feet smell. Though rennet is the vital substance that helps to create curds, bacteria are a big part of what make cheese taste good. Many modern cheesemakers begin the process by adding commercially produced cultures of starter bacteria to their milk. Traditionally, however, the starter bacteria came from the cheesemaking environment; they lived in the wooden buckets and paddles, or were added to fresh milk in the form of whey left over from the previous day's cheesemaking. As the cheese ages, enzymes produced by the bacteria break down the fats and proteins into fatty and amino acids, which are further broken down into smaller chemical components, all with various aromas and flavors. Hence cheese that can taste like burnt toast or smell like caramelized onions. Amino acids can also be converted into ammonia, which is why an overripe cheese sometimes gives off a whiff of Windex.

Then there are the things that grow on the outside. With many cheeses, cheesemakers ecourage molds to form a hard rind. The rind of a washed cheese, however, is made by coaxing the *Brevibacterium linens* to multiply. The cheeses receive regular wipe-downs with brine, which is sometimes mixed with bits of older cheeses to enrich the bacterial stew, and oftentimes fortified by spirits such as cider, beer, or the clear, colorless fruit brandy known as marc. The *Brevibacteria* give the cheeses a distinctive reddish to reddish-orange cast and a sticky, shiny finish, as if they're covered in clear-coat varnish that isn't quite dry. The rind of a Tamié, for instance, is a lustrous, vivid saffron. And it has a delicate toe-jam scent.

Foot odor notwithstanding, rind-washed cheeses usually taste far better than you'd expect—they can be almost steak-like, no doubt part of the appeal for monks abstaining from meat. Such a cheese could contribute significantly to the power of a religious order—which in turn furthered the spread of the cheese, to the point that a cheesemaking monastery could influence the *fromage* eaten throughout an entire region. This was the case with the hamlet of Maroilles, located in the northeast corner of France.

In 652, a Benedictine order founded an abbey there, and it's thought that a monk invented Maroilles cheese around the year 960 (a celebratory millennial Mass was held in 1960). Under the abbey's sway, the cheese spread so far and wide among the peasantry that even today almost all the cheeses of this part of France are derivatives of Maroilles. Besides Maroilles itself, there's the Boulette d'Avesnes, also known as *le suppositoire du diable*— "the devil's suppository"—which is made of leftover scraps of Maroilles molded into a cone shape and covered in paprika. Or another called Vieux Lille, which is Maroilles left to age well past its normal stench into something so deeply malodorous that the French have nicknamed it *le puant*—"the stinker." In fact, if you're in those parts and someone serves you a big, old smelly cheese, all you need say is "Maroilles," and chances are you'll be more than half right.

"Uncyclopedia," an online spoof of Wikipedia, jokes that cheese has been the currency used in Wisconsin since the Free Coinage of Cheese Act of 1912, but in reality cheese has long been used as money—and has long led to corruption. In Maroilles the monks used their cheese-fed dominance to tighten their grip on the area, claiming lands because they "belonged to God" and imposing on peasants a tax of one Maroilles cheese per cow per year. As it grew in influence, the abbey, like most powerful monasteries of its time, played host to a number of kings—and so a cheese's association with God sometimes led to an association with nobility (a connection so important that even today anyone wanting to say how superior a cheese is will liken it to royalty). The list of distinguished guests includes kings Philippe Auguste, Louis IX, Charles IV, François I, and Louis XIV, to name only a few. During these monarchs' visits the monks, of course, gave them Maroilles to eat. While not exactly like the current practice of designers' showering celebrities with free clothes and handbags, the effect was similar, at least insofar as it continued to spread a cheese's fame. For its more prestigious admirers, a Maroilles could even be personalized with an impression of their coat of arms on its surface.

The best-known story of monks and kings and cheese, however, involves not Maroilles, but the Abbaye de Conques in southern France. It was here that one day Charlemagne stopped while traveling and was served a curious cheese—not rind-washed but, rather, covered in a strange blue mold. Naturally he took up his knife to remove the mold, but a monk stopped him and urged him to eat the cheese as it was, blue flecks and all. The cheese, as you might guess, was what we now know as Roquefort. Though it had originated some fifty miles from the abbey, in the *caves* of the Combalou Mountain, Roquefort was already so widely renowned by the eleventh century that the monks collected a two-cheese rent from each hut producing the cheese. And with Charlemagne's support, the *bleu* would travel even farther: the ruler liked Roquefort so much that he ordered the abbey to supply his table with two mule loads of the stuff every year.

If you were a Roquefort maker, the news that your cheese graced the table of a king was likely cause for celebration. But fame and popularity inevitably come with challenges, and this soon enough proved to be the case for the Roquefort makers. Not only were people clambering to eat their cheeses, but they were also making cheeses that looked like the Roquefort makers' cheeses and calling them Roquefort. The situation became alarming enough that, in 1411, Roquefort makers secured from Charles VI an official monopoly on making the cheese. Thus began the first rudimentary attempts at gaining legal protection for a French food product. The name-control system wasn't an instant success—a couple of centuries later, faux Roqueforts remained enough of a menace that makers sought a decree by the Parlement de Toulouse reaffirming that the only real Roquefort was that aged in the Combalou Mountain. However, as more and more food producers demanded it, the early forms of government protection evolved into the modern system of AOCs that now safeguards everything from French figs to lentils, along with forty-some *fromages* and counting.

Back in Maroilles, meanwhile, relations between cheesemaking peasants and their rulers were less than amicable. Matters came to a head with the French Revolution, which brought a definitive end to the abbey's power and to much of the abbey itself: only a handful of structures survives today, including the abbey's waterwheel, which continues to churn placidly at the village's entrance, and the cheese *caves* (still used to age Maroilles).

A signpost on the former grounds explains that the group of *pay-sans* who stormed the abbey in 1791 and set off the subsequent dismantling had rallied about the cry *"Non au fromage à la vache!"* which roughly translates to "We won't pay your stinking cheese tax no more, you fat, rich monks!"

BUT HOWEVER MUCH a cheese might have been associated with the Divine, something more powerful than God fires the gastronomic passions of most French people. Or, at least, this is what most of them would say. I am talking, *bien sûr,* about *terroir.*

At its most basic, *terroir* means "dirt"—a small word for a big idea. One of the reasons France has so many cheeses is because its landscapes are so varied: plains and mountains, river deltas and swamps, seacoasts and deserts. Each of these niche environments has its particular soil composition and bacterial strains— its own *terroir.* The taste of a cheese starts with its *terroir,* just as with a wine, and the animals drawing nourishment from the earth are rather like the vines in winemaking. *Terroir* is a somewhat slippery concept when it comes to *fromage*—as a French friend pointed out to me, cows have feet and vines do not. Still, food writer Eric LeMay wasn't far off when he said that you can pretty much think of cows as big, walking grapes.

Hand in hand with a region's soil, climate and topography also affected how people went about making their cheese. In mountainous regions such as Auvergne, people had to stockpile enough cheese to get them through the long winters, so they used the bountiful summer milk to make hard cheeses that could be aged and stored for upward of a year. If trees were sparse in the hills, people pressed their cheeses, and if trees were plentiful, they took advantage of the ready fuel and cooked them first. In the warmer lowlands, where animals could graze nearly year-round, people tended to make smaller, softer cheeses, aging them anywhere from a few days to a few months. There was, of course, considerable crossover. In months when milking was starting up or tapering off and there wasn't enough milk for a big cheese, mountain peoples made smaller cheeses; in months when they had a lot of milk, lowlanders would sometimes make hard cheeses. And all cheesemakers had some sort of *fromage frais*. If you have curds lying around, why not eat them?

Nearly every region of France also used to have its particular cow, not unlike the different *cépages*—"grape varieties"—in winemaking, and each gave a slightly different milk. Charming as this sounds, an area's native breed might be too temperamental to keep (Salers cows being an excellent example) or, worse yet, might not yield a lot of milk. So breeds that do produce good yields, such as Holsteins—the ubiquitous black-and-white-splotched breed in Wisconsin pastures that I knew as a kid—have taken over cheesemaking in many places. They're so popular, in fact, that a number of the old French breeds have gone extinct. The French blame this plague of Holsteins on Americans: even though the breed was originally Dutch, the stock has become largely North American. (William Howard Taft even kept a Holstein, named Pauline Wayne, as the White House pet.)

Of course, cows, though hugely present in France—eight million calves are born every year, outnumbering human newborns ten to one—are just one sort of animal used to make cheese. Just as some areas are better suited for certain cultivars of grape, some places are better suited for certain animals. Goats and sheep can survive in rocky, arid locales where a cow would starve. Not only do they require less food, but their diet is more varied: goats will scarf some 460 different plant species, whereas cows restrict themselves to around 330. So what kind of animal you kept had a lot to do with what kind of animal could thrive in your *terroir*. This makes the process sound rather deliberate, as if the ancient tribes of France might have ordered goats off the Internet because they had a nice patch of ground perfect for goats, but in reality, animals moved around with human populations and the sort you ended up with was partly a matter of serendipity.

The Loire Valley and most of southwestern France, for instance, is famous goat cheese territory because when the Saracens invaded France in the eighth century, they brought their goats with them. The goats thrived so well that people held on to them even after the Saracens had been driven out, and the invaders' Moorish roots can still be detected in the name of a log-shaped goat cheese from the Loire: St. Maure de Touraine, or "St. Moor." Why "Saint" Maure, I can't say, given that the

Arabs were enemies—unless it's a reference to how the goats have proved useful for more than cheese from time to time. On one such occasion, in 1569, a group of besieged villagers near the hamlet of Nontron tied lengths of oil- and tar-soaked hemp to the tails of their goats, set them afire after nightfall, and sent them running through a camp of invading Huguenots. The Huguenots, waking to this vision of satanic demons, immediately fled.

Such a defense, although no doubt rare in French history, suggests what life was like in what were then the wilds of France. We're accustomed to thinking of France as one big *pays*—"country"—but a Frenchwoman living prior to the French Revolution would not have seen it this way. Individuals did not live in "France"; they lived in their own, Lilliputian-size *pays,* each corresponding roughly to the area in which the parish church bell could be heard. Most people spent their entire lives within earshot of that bell, and other than religion, few things had greater influence over their lives, and what cheese they made, than their *pays.* Those few who traveled among these "spheres of audible influence" often found themselves engaging in extreme ethnography, as described by historian and author Graham Robb: "On fording a stream or turning at a crossroads, the occupants of a carriage could find themselves among people of radically different appearance, with their own style of dress and architecture, their own language and their own peculiar concept of hospitality." Only after the Revolution—when Parisian administrators sliced up the country with little regard for the old boundaries and imposed an ambitious educational system of French language and culture on the general population—did something resembling modern France begin to emerge. This was the "puzzle of micro-provinces," Robb explains, "that General de Gaulle had in mind when he asked, 'How can one be expected to govern a country that has two hundred and forty-six different kinds of cheese?'"

So people took what they had—the land, the climate, the animals—and, in the relative isolation of their *pays,* shaped their cheeses into something unique. This is *terroir*: a concept much larger than dirt. A French friend once sent me writings on the subject by Hippocrates, who described certain peoples "who resemble mountainous terrain," and others who resembled "marshes," and still others who were like "dry, desolate plains." The same friend also sent along a somewhat unusual but telling definition of *terroir*: "the rural region considered to be the cause of the particular character of its inhabitants." It is not, in other words, the people who shape the land, but the land that shapes the people. Though it might be truer to say it's a cycle—the land shapes the people and then the people shape the land, and then all of it shapes the cheeses. Throw in some monks and the odd king or two, and you have the passion-inspiring existence, in France, of so much more than just one nice cheddar.

3

A LITTLE GOAT CHEESE

~~~~~~~~~

"Each sort of cheese reveals a pasture of a different green,
under a different sky."

—ITALO CALVINO

If you were a peasant living on the edge of the Causse de
Gramat in southwestern France, the best thing you could
have was a goat. The only thing better than a goat might be
two or three goats. A cow was costly not only to buy, but to
keep. Your goats, however, could survive on the grasses and
wildflowers—toadflax, milk vetch, bindweed, knapweed—that
grew in sparse tufts between scrubby junipers. They would even
happily eat the bark of the trees that huddled in the basin of any
slight slope. The Causse de Gramat might be classified as a lesser
causse—the limestone plateaux become progressively higher and

more jagged farther to the east—but life here was harsh enough. The parched shelf of the *causse* had once been covered by an inland sea, which must have made what little water that did fall seem ironic. It was also ephemeral: when it rained, storms glazed the fossil-encrusted limestone with droplets that disappeared so swiftly they might have been falling on a giant colander.

You would have spent much of your day occupied with rocks—turning them up with plows, piling them in heaps, building them into walls or shelters or niches for beehives—so many rocks that you and the other peasants would say the earth grew them. If you happened to be a nursing mother, the hours of hard labor could have caused you to lose your milk, and then your goat might have saved your baby's life. Because it has smaller fat globules than cow's milk, goat's milk is easier to digest, making it the preferred substitute for human milk. You wouldn't even have needed a bottle, because the child could have suckled directly from the udder. This practice continued well into the mid-nineteenth century: In 1852 a doctor in central France wrote of holding his infant twins under the family's goat, which had become so used to the task that "she has arrived at jumping on the bed to get to the suckling babies faster." If you were a peasant who lived near Paris rather than in the *causses,* you might even have earned a few coins by bringing your goat wet nurse directly to the doorsteps of city dwellers.

But the very best thing about your goat was that you could have used the milk to make cheese. This is what one of those peasants, Justine Carbonié, did on a farm on the Causse de Gramat starting in the late 1800s. In French, any goat's milk cheese can be called a *chèvre* (though it's worth bearing in mind that the female animal giving the milk is *la chèvre* while the cheeses go by the masculine *le chèvre*—a distinction particularly important in a cheese shop, where it's best not to ask for *la chèvre* unless you're hoping the shopkeeper might produce a live female goat). But Justine's cheeses, true to the place that formed her, were called *cabécou,* from Occitan, the old language of the south. *Cabé* means "goat," while *cou* is the diminutive, so from her goats Justine and other women like her made bunches of "little goats."

At Justine's farm, now called La Borie d'Imbert, large sepia images of Justine and her husband, Janissou, are omnipresent, adorning signage and flanking the doorway of a fieldstone building that houses a ticket counter and gift shop. The couple looks reliably stout and nearly expressionless in the way of all people photographed in the early twentieth century. Of the two, it was Justine, with her sacklike dress and sagging breasts, who caught my gaze: There was something in the way she held herself, in the blunt rounding of her shoulders and the slight, almost wry line of her lips that made me feel wistful and almost sad. Here was the face of Old France, of cheesemaking before the modern era came along and complicated matters. Justine's former farmstead has been turned into a living museum, complete with a restored farmhouse, barn, outbuildings, pigeon coop, bread oven, rock-walled pastures, and vineyards. Geese and other fowl peck gravel, rabbits stock the hatches, tender herbs and vegetables sprout in the *potager*—and on the day I visited, I turned a corner outside the house to find a large, very pink pig lolling in the mud. This is where Justine lived out her days. Here she tended her garden, her flocks, and her goats. She made her cheeses.

Still, though she made cheese, Justine would not have thought of herself as a cheesemaker, or at least not exclusively as such. For most *fromagères* in France at the turn of the nineteenth century, cheesemaking was just one of many farm tasks that shaped the rhythms of life, and her *terroir* shaped her without her conscious awareness. In the late winter and early spring, when her goats gave birth and began giving milk, she commenced the summertime work of making cheese. The cheeses were small and round—just a couple of inches across and half an inch high—because small and round was a shape the local metalworkers knew how to make. On the day I visited, I spied an oil lamp fixed to the wall near a bed in Justine's restored farmhouse; its metal base was nearly the exact size and shape of a *cabécou* mold.

Justine made cheeses primarily for the family, and in fact might not even have cared overmuch whether they tasted good. For most farmwives, the most important characteristic of their cheeses was that they kept well. If they didn't taste good, so much the better: that meant the family went through fewer of them. But I like to believe that Justine cared, that she made her family the best cheeses she knew how. In times when she had more *fromages* than they could possibly eat—such as in the early summer, when the grasses were flush and the goats gave lots of rich milk—she filled a wooden carrier with *cabécou,* covered in a scrap of linen to keep the flies away, and toted it to market, where she could earn herself some pin money.

From the comfortable distance of a hundred years, this all sounds lovely and bucolic, and perhaps it was, at least some of the time. In reality, the lives of French peasants were filled with quiet tragedy, and Justine certainly knew her share. Two of the four sons she had with Janissou died in infancy. The other two were killed in World War I, one at the age of twenty-one and the other at twenty-two. No matter how unsentimental her lot might have made her, the grief must have been almost unbearable.

Justine's farm happens to lie not far from the edge of the town of Rocamadour, a famous pilgrimage site on the route of Saint Jacques de Compostelle. The town was originally settled by a band of scruffy hermits who sheltered under a sheer cliff face—the *roc*—and worshipped the Virgin Mary. Since the mid-twelfth century, when what was thought to be the well-preserved body of Amadour, one of the hermits, was found during church construction, Rocamadour has been a destination for generations of souls looking for solace of one kind or another. The most devout ascended the Great Stairway to the shrine on their knees, dragging themselves over marine fossils embedded in the treads. After her children died, maybe Justine climbed those stairs, just as the pilgrims did, then continued upward along a serpentine course, praying at each station as she made her way to a giant cross at the top. I picture Justine mourning her sons in its shadow, perhaps little knowing that she was also mourning the passing of an entire way of life: For not only had she and Janissou lost their boys, they'd also lost their laborers. It was a tragedy that repeated itself throughout the continent as the Great War nearly wiped out an entire generation.

THE POSTWAR YEARS would witness other, more heartening developments in the world of *fromage*. It's not impossible that Justine might have seen a sign of this herself. Perhaps one day, while she was out tending the geese or pulling weeds from around her tarragon, she might have looked up to see a young man riding down the unpaved road trailing a cloud of dust. Perhaps he left his bicycle at the gate, doffing his beret and slapping it against his thigh to dislodge the grit as he approached. He was slight, with dark hair and a mustache. Nor had he escaped the war unscathed, having lost an eye in battle. As he walked to greet Justine, maybe he reminded her of her less-fortunate sons. If that young man did arrive at Justine's farm on this hypothetical morning, he would have told her his name was Henri Androuët, and that he was looking for cheese.

Henri was born one of eight children in Brittany. In 1900 he left home to try his luck in Paris, where he worked his way up from cleaning stables to making deliveries in a horse and buggy for the French food firm Gervais. On his rounds, he met Ida, a pretty maiden who worked in a small store that sold butter, eggs, and cheese. They soon married and went into debt to buy the shop. Then came the war, from which Henri returned in late 1914 not only half-blind, but also suffering from headaches and mood swings that would affect him for the rest of his life. These ailments, however, apparently did not prevent him from attending to certain matrimonial duties—their son, Pierre, was born in August of 1915. When not procreating, Henri spent his long convalescence thinking of ways to improve his and Ida's little shop. He was dissatisfied with the cheeses then available at Les Halles, the wholesale market in Paris's first arrondissement. Known as "the stomach" of Paris, Les Halles was a sprawling affair composed of a dozen glass and iron pavilions that had been designed by architect Victor Baltard in the mid- to late 1800s. No matter its prodigious size and glitz, though, many of the merchants did not offer more than a handful of cheeses. *Fromage,* for most, was something of a sideline, and the few cheeses on offer arrived mostly overripe and damaged from the countryside. Henri thought he could do better.

As soon as he was able, he boarded a train, taking the rails as far as they would go into various regions, where he visited local wholesalers and middlemen. Then, having toured the village *marché*—"the market"—he'd set out on his bicycle to find the farmers themselves. It seems sensible that if you want the best cheeses, you should seek them out at their source, but before Henri came along, no one had thought to do so. Once he'd tracked down the best cheesemakers, he arranged to have them send young cheeses to the city, where he could oversee their aging himself, in *caves* below his shop. Nobody had thought to do that before, either. Henri was, it turns out, inventing the métier of the *fromager affineur*—those clever individuals who do not merely sell cheeses, but who understand and promote the best of them.

Henri began to concentrate exclusively on cheese; by 1926 *la maison* Androuët was stocking more than a hundred varieties—an unheard-of number. Henri also began to produce folding calendars for his Parisian customers that included information on the weird delicacies occupying the wooden *planches* of his *cave*: where the cheeses came from, and the time of year when each would be *en pleine maturité*. The calendars proved an enormous success, and their legacy lives on in the "From'Girls" calendars produced by the Association Fromages de Terroirs, an advocacy group for traditional French cheese (though, with aims that are rather less educational: the modern calendars feature cheeses Photoshopped into images of scantily clad women). Eventually Henri opened a room next to his *cave* for *dégustations,* where people came to sit at tables covered in striped cotton cloth, surrounded by *fromage*-filled wooden shelves, and speared hunks of cheese for themselves on the tip of a knife. By the 1930s Henri's son, Pierre, a former student of architecture, began to take an interest in the family business, drawing up plans for a restaurant. The new *resto* soon attracted bevies of cheese lovers, including Ernest Hemingway, Paul Brach, Orson Welles, and French novelist and provocateur Colette, who signed the establishment's *livre d'or* with a warning to young women: "Beware of men who like neither wine, music or cheese." The roster also included Maria Callas, who liked to go into the kitchen to make her own scrambled eggs and cheese.

Unless they happened to be produced close to Paris or in fairly large operations, most French cheeses had languished in relative obscurity until Henri Androuët came along. He helped bring the country cheeses of France into the light, taking them from their rustic birthplaces and displaying them in the windows of his shop in Paris. And his son, Pierre—the one who became known as the "pope" of French cheese—would help to make them known around the world.

IF HENRI HAD come to Justine Carbonié's farmhouse door, it's hard to know what, if anything, she might have made of him and his cheese-seeking. Hard to know what her daily life was like, hard to know how she felt about cheese—if, indeed, she felt anything about it at all. Justine and her fellow *fromagères* are long gone. Still, a version of her persists in the French countryside. They might be fewer and farther between now than they were in her time, but farmwives across France still make goat cheeses, and they still take their cheeses to market.

• • •

ON A BRISK spring day, I stood with one of them, a woman named Monique Marsat, watching her goats nibble hay. Overhead, droplets spattered the barn roof's thick plastic sheeting. "They don't like the rain," Monique commented, and I nodded. The window of the bed-and-breakfast room I had in the house overlooked the back of the barn and pasture, and I'd spent much of the past few days watching the goats hie in and out in time to the bursts of spring showers. *"Des Alpines polychromes,"* Monique said with a teasing smile when I asked about the goats' breed—"polychromatic Alpines." I could see why she called them that. The goats were mostly chestnut and black, though some had splotches of creamy fur, and some were speckled with beige. "Usually Alpines are chestnut with black along the spine, but for a long time now I've picked goats for their color and beauty, not for their milk," Monique explained. "When I started out they were all the standard chestnut, but as soon as I had one with a little splotch, poof! I kept it." She chuckled. "I don't like uniformity," she said. "Though, of course, they do still have to produce milk."

With her husband, Didier, Monique owns a farm known as the Ferme de Poutignac, half a day's drive to the north of the *causses*. The farm is in the Dordogne, a lushly forested region where images of grandmothers force-feeding ducks for foie gras are still considered quaint. The farmstead itself was a tumble of meandering buildings that managed to seem at once both solid and about to crumble into picturesque ruin. The farmhouse looked as though it had been stuck together out of three or four buildings, each made from a different material: stucco, dressed stone, fieldstone, cement block. It and the various garages and outbuildings were topped by tile roofs fleeced with lichen. Inside, the living area featured shelves lined with books, trailing pothos plants, quilts hanging on the walls, and a lime-green coffeemaker. On the patch of lawn in front of a set of French doors, Monique had planted rosemary and assorted flowers in wooden barrels, beside a table and chairs in curlicued wrought iron. Just up the lane was the fifteenth-century château where, in former times, the lord would have lived. It now bore a sign on its gate that read, "Chien Méchant"—"Mean Dog."

Monique is fiftyish, with short-cropped sandy-blond hair. She and Didier have been raising goats for over thirty years. I could easily picture her as a twentysomething with long, super-flat hair parted down the middle and a daisy stuck behind one ear. In some ways, Monique, part of the disaffected, post-'68 generation that drifted to the countryside in search of the authentic, isn't at all like Justine. She and Didier decided to go into goats while on holiday together in Greece in 1974. At the time, she'd been studying literature in England while he worked for auto manufacturer Citroën in Paris. "We saw goats in the Greek countryside, and we said, 'That's what we're going to do.' " They came back to France, married, and began their herd. "Back then it was still easy to get started in goat farming with very little.

Goats weren't very expensive. You could buy a baby goat, and at the end of six months they were ready to breed, so you would have another goat by the following spring. And in a year, a goat will produce enough milk to pay for itself. *La chèvre c'était la vache du pauvre,*" she said, repeating the old saying for me—"The goat was the cow of the poor."

Yet, in other ways, she's just like Justine. There's a reason the Latin word for goat, *capra,* is to be found at the root of the word *capricious.* Adaptable and sturdy though they are, goats can also be difficult creatures, a difficulty that extends to their lactation cycle. Those of us who didn't grow up on farms can sometimes forget that in order to give milk, an animal must first give birth. With a cow, this isn't much of a problem—cows will produce young no matter the month, meaning that cow's-milk cheeses can be available year-round. Goats, however, are rather less amenable. If left to their own devices, they give birth in late winter or early spring, then give milk through the summer months and into the fall. In the winter, they go dry. In Justine's time, of course, this meant that goat cheese appeared on the table only as the last dregs of winter washed themselves away. Such dewy rounds of *chèvre* used to herald spring across France.

Today, people want goat's-milk cheeses for their holiday parties in December. Certainly it's possible to age a fresh *chèvre.* At one promotional center (cheeses in France actually have such things), a woman offered me a shrunken, six-month-old Valençay. "You can still eat it?" I wondered aloud. "Oh yes," she'd said, industriously shaving a desiccated sliver from one side. But most people prefer their *chèvres* a tad more youthful. As a result, many larger makers, even traditional ones, now manipulate part of their herd into a fall birthing so that they can have fresh milk year-round. The animals are either given hormones or kept in a barn, where the light levels can be adjusted to fool them into thinking it's time to mate.

But not at the Marsats' farm: "We introduce the buck in the summer, and they do as they like," Monique said, waving a hand. In the barn were thirty or so *chevrettes,* the young born since January. In choosing to live with the seasons, Monique has chosen to live a life more like Justine's than that of many of her contemporaries. At the Ferme de Poutignac, the first goat cheeses of the year still arrive with the daffodils.

THE CHEESE MONIQUE makes is also *cabécou*—the same cheese Justine made, and very nearly the same cheese peasants of the Dordogne made for centuries. Her *fromagerie*—a word that can mean a shop where cheeses are sold, but also, as in this case, the cheesemaker's workshop—is housed in a stone outbuilding with clumps of grass and ivy lapping at its foundation. From the barn, we walked the short distance to the building along muddy, rain-wet tracks, chatting about Monique's early studies in English literature—she was a fan of the eighteenth-century pastoral-ist poet William Blake—then we climbed a set of rough-hewn steps and went through a white door. In the entryway to a room tiled in white, Monique handed me a pair of blue booties to slip over my shoes while she donned a cloudy white lunch lady's bonnet and tied an apron over her plaid shirt. Inside the room, four white plastic buckets sat on an aluminum table.

The day before, Monique had added rennet to the milk in the buckets. Traditionally, rennet was produced by slaughtering a calf, drying its stomach, and then cutting said stomach into small pieces which were used to make a rennet solution. (If the thought of calf stomachs makes you squeamish, you should know that milk can also be curdled with plant or microbial agents. This method is relatively common in the United States, but in France, animal rennet must be used if you want to call your cheese cheese. By law, *fromage* made with other coagulating agents doesn't count.) Not only was the whole slaughtering-the-calf thing rather messy, but the resulting compound could vary in potency, making it hard to judge how much rennet to use. In the late 1800s, researchers managed to extract and stabilize rennet in a laboratory, creating a concentration that was not only constant, but also storable. Since then, Monique and others like her have been able to purchase commercially produced rennet, which has left them off the hook when it comes to personally killing baby animals.

After adding the rennet, Monique must leave her milk to sit unruffled in a warm spot, where it curdles in Zen-like stillness for some twenty-four hours. After it reaches the proper consistency—a bit like thick yogurt—it's ready to be put into molds. It was at this stage now, and she tilted one bucket so that I could see the solid mass of curd beneath a thin layer of liquid. She grabbed a stack of round perforated containers made of white plastic, about four inches across and five or so high. Then she took up a large slotted spoon, which she nestled into the curd before transferring the spoonful lightly into the mold, taking care to disturb the curd as little as possible. Since most *chèvres* are soft cheeses, the curd must be scooped gently—"*doucement*," Monique said—so that it retains its moisture and smooth texture. "Can I try?" I asked. "Of course," Monique said, and moved over. The curd landed in the waiting mold with a soft plop. I tried to imagine doing the same thing over and over every morning, seven days a week from spring through fall. I could not. Though Monique now has a hired girl who helps some days, for many years she made all the cheeses herself.

I wondered aloud if Monique liked making cheese. In the past, goat cheese makers were typically female. (As one male *chèvre* producer told me, it wasn't "*très macho*" for men to be out messing around with delicate little goats.) In many places, this divide still holds: the wife makes cheese while the husband takes care of other farm tasks, especially those involving tractors. "Yes," Monique said, in answer to my question. "I put on France Culture [a sort of French version of NPR] or some music"—she gestured to a radio on a shelf in her workroom—"and I'm good." That morning, she'd been listening to a program about Jacques Brel, the Belgian singer-songwriter who wrote the original, French version of the 1970s hit "Seasons in the Sun."

I asked if we were making *cabécou,* but it turned out the molds were for what Monique calls *"un rond,"* meaning a button-like *chèvre* flecked with blue mold. "It's a penicillium mold," Monique noted, "the sort the Americans usually don't like." On a rack behind her sat a row of drying *bûches*—log-shaped cheeses—coated in the other sort of traditional coating Americans don't usually like: ash. A Frenchwoman I know who'd lived in the States once told me about hosting a tasting at which she had served Morbier, a cheese from the Jura that's bisected by a frayed, dark line of soot. When she told one young woman what the stripe was made of, the girl promptly spat her mouthful out.

Since most Americans are not in the habit of eating cinders, this reaction is understandable. As far as I'm aware, however, no one has ever died from eating ashes or any other cheese rind; eating it is less a matter of safety than of personal taste. I, for one, avoid the tough rind of hard, aged cheeses (though there are French people who profess to like it), but I find trying to cut away the skinlike rind of a beautifully mold-covered soft cheese not only difficult but also wasteful. As for soot-covered goat cheeses, *fromagers* in the old days would take real wood ash from the *cul*—"ass"—of a kettle hanging over the hearth and sprinkle it on new cheeses to keep the flies off. Now they use commercially produced vegetable ash instead. Like those activated charcoal tablets people take to aid digestion, it has no taste or smell, and is perfectly sterile and harmless.

There is one type of rind, however, that I do advise against eating. When you see a pocked, cratered, and dusty rind, two words should come to mind: cheese mites. The mites, which are microscopic, creep into the cheesemaking *caves* because they like dark, out-of-the-way places. This doesn't mean you shouldn't eat such cheeses: the mites are considered part of the aging process, and *affineurs* actually manage their growth by regularly brushing the rinds (too many mites and you no longer have cheese; you have something inedible). All of this, of course, is because the mites are believed to improve flavor. A good example is Mimolette, an orange, ball-shaped *fromage.* I've had young Mimolette, before the mites have really done their work, and I've had Mimolette *extra vieille,* presumably after the mites have vacated. The young one was practically tasteless, while the aged Mimolette tasted amazing: intensely nutty and caramely. (If you think cheese mites sound bad, consider a cheese from Corsica called Appignato, which is traditionally aged in earthenware containers until suitably infested with maggots. Patrick Rance writes of seeing one: "not so much a moveable as a moving feast." These days the Corsican variety is hard to come by, although rumor has it you can still find another, well-known "maggot cheese" from Sardinia, the Italian island just to the south. It's called Casu Marzu, and people scarfing down the delicacy are said to wear eye protection because the little buggers can jump.)

In addition to the vexation posed by rinds, would-be *chèvre* connoisseurs also confront the difficulty of all their names. Goat cheeses are the modeling clay of the cheese world, capable of taking scores of different forms, the words for which then often become their handles. These forms traditionally varied by region. In one place, the *chèvres* might be squarish like cobblestones; in another, they look like bells; in another, like pears or hearts or shamrocks. Such shape-shifting is all fine, if a bit cutesy, until you reach a cheese that looks like a tiny penis, the literal translation for T'chiot Biloute, a variety from the north of France (it's technically a cow's-milk cheese, but the name is still funny, and I wouldn't be surprised if someone somewhere in France were selling a *chèvre* called "little penis"), or a *crottin*— "turd." Today *crottins* are usually eaten while still quite young and white in color, but in previous times they were sometimes left to dry to a decidedly poo-like shade. One *chèvre* maker whom I spoke with tried to convince me the word had come from an old type of farmhouse terra-cotta oil lamp, though Rance sniffed at such attempts to find a "more genteel derivation of Crottin." "My guess," he concluded, is that "the oil lamps were named for the same reason that the cheeses were: they looked like horse dung."

In order to get the *cabécou* shape, Monique first ladles curd onto a piece of mesh set into a basket, where it has to drain for another twenty-four hours. Then she carefully mixes salt into the curd, rather than coating the cheese in salt after taking it from the mold, as is the case with most *chèvres*. Salt affects the taste of a *chèvre* quite a lot, so the savoir faire of the cheesemaker is important. Then she uses a rectangle of heavy metal with rows of round, *cabécou*-shaped holes die-cut into it—rather like a bottomless muffin pan. She scooped some curd into the holes to show me, then lifted away the metal rectangle to reveal neat rows of baby *cabécous* ready for aging. Once the aging is complete, Monique will trundle them to the nearby open-air market in Villebois-Lavalette, where she sells them under a covered wooden pavilion very similar to the kind that stood there in medieval times. It's a romantic sort of thing to do, but then, Monique is a romantic sort.

Later that evening, I would sit in my room with one of Monique's *cabécous* warm in my palm. It was pale—the *pâte* of a *chèvre* is lighter in color than a cow's-milk cheese because goats convert more carotene (which, as you may recall from middle school science class, is what makes carrots orange) to vitamin A—and it was lovely. In my hand it felt sort of fleshy, almost alive, and when I squeezed it, the firmer *pâte* slid about in the little pouch made by the *croûte*. I cut it open with my Swiss army knife, and a layer of cream oozed about the edges. When I put my nose down to it and sniffed, it smelled heavenly, like the moist hay of the goat barn. Then I cut a morsel and placed it on my tongue. The taste was grassy and lemony, almost to the point of being tangy. There was salt, too, and a pleasant, musky aftertaste. It was the taste of Poutignac, of the farmhouse in the early morning light, of the polychromatic goats in the barn, of wildflowers like those Monique had hand-painted onto the tiles in my little bathroom, carefully writing their Latin names—*Viola odorata* or

Primula veris—underneath each picture. The cheese seemed almost a part of Monique herself.

AT THE SAME time, Monique's *cabécous* aren't just hers. They're what's properly known as Cabécou de Périgord, which is the old name, in Occitan, for Dordogne. "It's a *marque déposée*," she said, meaning the name is trademarked, but not quite an AOC yet. (As one writer put it, France has a "veritable caste system" of appellations. Others include the Label Rouge and the OGP, as well as the *Appellation d'Origine Protégée,* or AOP, essentially an AOC at the level of the European Union. As AOC is still the term most people are familiar with, I've stuck to that designation to avoid confusion.) The concept of appellations began, of course, with Roquefort in the late Middle Ages. But the modern AOC system didn't truly start until 1919, with the Law for the Protection of the Place of Origin, a piece of legislation aimed at protecting vineyards, which were then still recovering from the phylloxera epidemic that devastated France's wine industry in the latter half of the nineteenth century.

For the first few decades, the AOC designation was reserved mostly for wines. Still, as early as the 1920s and '30s, some French people were concerned that traditional food products might also be threatened by modern developments. Not only had World War I wreaked its havoc on the rural population, but scientists had also produced some much-lauded, and potentially alarming, advances over the preceding fifty years. Chief among these scientists, of course, was one Louis Pasteur. Pasteur's research had focused on preventing wine and beer from going bad, but his disciples would soon enough apply his theories to cheese. In 1900, Pierre Mazé, who had studied with the microbiologist Émile Duclaux (he of cheese classification fame), helped found a laboratory dedicated to the improvement of cheeses. By the 1910s the laboratory's work was opening the door to pasteurization in *fromageries*. The researchers were also isolating useful strains of bacteria that could be cultivated in the lab, then used to inseminate cheeses. Before, cheesemakers had relied on whatever bacteria were naturally present in the *fromageries* and cheese *caves,* which sometimes yielded results that were not only undesirable, but inedible. The laboratory cultures allowed for much more control and uniformity. Some early twentieth-century French observers of the cheese trade felt so emboldened by the advances as to claim that any sort of cheese could be made anywhere. *Terroir,* it was whispered, didn't matter.

Along with the science were advances in technology: electricity, steam-driven cheese presses, temperature-controlled rooms for aging—that is to say, the first stirring of industrial cheese, with the Roquefort producers leading the way. Ever mindful of the need to protect the Roquefort name, they petitioned for and, in 1925, won the first official AOC to be granted to a cheese. Few cheesemakers of the time could claim to be quite so organized. Efforts by producers of other *fromages* to get similar protection were haphazard and slow. For a quarter of a century, Roquefort would remain the only cheese to have legal protection. And even close to one hundred years later, some cheesemakers—including producers of Cabécou du Périgord—are still working toward an AOC.

The exact meaning and purpose of that legal protection aren't as obvious as they might appear. Like most Americans, I'd always taken the French AOC label on my food as a guarantee that that food had been made in accordance with tradition. Your average French person, it seems, has similar notions. Early in my research, I'd picked up a copy of *Vie Pratique Santé*—or *Practical Health*—magazine while standing in the checkout line at a *supermarché*. An article called "50 Truths About Dairy Products" explained that AOC products "come from a defined *terroir,* as do their ingredients, and are made using traditional savoir faire." But I had already begun to suspect that the function of an AOC might be far more complicated. After all, the early Roquefort producers clearly had interests other than tradition in mind back in the Middle Ages when they first asked rulers to make it illegal for competitors to use their name.

Monique began to confirm my inkling, describing the first wrinkle in the AOC process: "You have to define each characteristic of the cheese," she explained, and then bring together all the producers to sign off on the description. Even though these different producers might all make a cheese they call *cabécou,* each might use a slightly different technique and each might produce a *cabécou* a little bit smaller or a little bit taller. But an AOC cheese cannot be "too diverse," and so much of the discussion between producers centers on the "harmonization" of techniques. Once the appellation goes through, everyone wanting to make the cheese will have to use the same molds in order to ensure that their cheeses match the shape and size laid out in what's known as the *cahier des charges*. Those who don't conform won't be allowed to label their cheeses "Cabécou du Périgord"—even if they come from families that have been making Cabécou in Périgord for generations.

In order to preserve France's diversity of traditional cheeses, that is, the AOC begins by making them less diverse. I asked Monique, she of the many-colored goats, what she thought about that. "It's admittedly difficult," she said, "to untangle the needs of the group and the needs of each individual producer. But in order to develop a bit more, in order to sell a bit farther away, in order to have the product be economically viable, you must arrive, all the same, at a production that resembles that of other makers. So we make geographic zones and find techniques in common. My cheeses don't taste the same as my neighbors' cheeses, but they will have the same format—the same shape. And they'll have the same milk—goat's milk, that is—and we'll use the same technology to make them. I'll add my rennet when my milk is at the same temperature, I'll mold up the curd twenty-four hours later in the same type of molds. But even so, the taste of each maker's cheese will be different.

"If everyone works in this same way, you have cheeses that are not the same, but that look similar and that can carry an image farther away. It's a balance. And even though I don't like controls . . ." She paused. "But still, it's necessary if you want a product that can go farther than the village down the road." And besides, she said, "The French love their AOCs."

BACK IN JUSTINE'S time, of course, most cheeses never did go much farther than the village down the road. Fresh goat cheeses, in particular, were difficult to ship, and unless there was someone like a Henri Androuët making the effort to get them into the city, they stayed put. Visiting the home of one goat cheese maker, I saw a watercolor painting of a teeny old woman in a white blouse, blue skirt, and straw hat sitting on a folding stool amid seven goats, her knitting needles at hand. I could imagine Justine sitting just that way, tending her goats as best she could as the years ticked by, tending them even after the death of Janissou in 1938, even as the news of yet another war began to penetrate *la France profonde*. She would have been an old woman, then, nearly eighty, in a country that was about to see its biggest change yet.

Justine died in the early 1950s, but the night before I left Poutignac, I had the curious sensation that I could almost catch a glimpse of the France she lived in, the one passing away alongside her. I took a walk along the tree-lined road near the farm.

As I strolled, I ran into a woman puffing a cigarette and wearing a belted navy dress that looked like it could have come straight from 1944. There was something else, too, something about the sagging stone house from which she'd emerged, and the muted edge to the twilight air, maybe, that made me think of the light and color in an old film. As she called out a throaty greeting, I somehow half-expected to see Allied troops tromping into sight from around the next bend.

CHEESE IS A BATTLEFIELD

~~~~~~~~~

"A cheese may disappoint. It may be dull, it may be
naïve, it may be oversophisticated. Yet it remains cheese,
milk's leap toward immortality."

—CLIFTON FADIMAN

At slightly before eight on Wednesday, June 14, 1944,
the coming day in Vimoutiers must still have held the
freshly laundered feel of a morning barely begun. In the center of town the two fairy-tale spires of the neo-Gothic church
of Notre Dame de Vimoutiers punctuated a sky of intense blue
softened by a few gauzy clouds. Across from the church, in the
village square, a sunlit monument to heroes of the Great War—
topped by France's national bird, the rooster—stood against a
line of espaliered trees bushy with tender leaves. The air was

abuzz with the hope of liberation from the Germans who were then stationed in towns and bunkers throughout Normandy. A little over a week earlier, on June 6, Allied forces had landed on beaches nearby, not even fifty miles from the threshold of the church. Freedom seemed imminent.

A noise broke the usual morning sounds that might have been heard: birds twittering, people coming and going on the square, the splash of water as a man rinsed the pavement in front of his café. The distant drone grew louder, resolving into the sound of many planes, until, all at once, nearly thirty B-26 bombers were passing overhead in precise formation—the Americans! They made one majestic sweep over the village, the D-day invasion stripes painted on their wings glinting as they banked in the morning light. Below them, on the square, in the streets, before the church, people would have craned their heads to watch, hearts rising to bob in the wake of their flight. And then the planes began to drop their bombs.

The bombing had been ordered based on what would turn out to be mistaken intelligence, but this didn't keep the half-timbered buildings surrounding the square from collapsing, didn't stop the shattering of the church's rose window, didn't save the world from bursting into flame. When the smoke cleared, it revealed a fuming landscape of rubble punctuated by the blackened spines of chimneys. The bombardment lasted fifteen minutes. It killed more than two hundred people and nearly leveled the town.

Over the next few days, dazed survivors assembled a make-shift hospital and began to pick through the wreckage. Just two days before the bombing, the tree-lined square would have brimmed with merchants' awnings and housewives filling wicker baskets with produce. Market day at Vimoutiers drew farmers from villages across the surrounding countryside, including the one a few miles down the road called Camembert. In the Halle au Beurre—"Butter Hall"—wholesalers would have been weighing slabs of butter the size of roasting pigs and buying round after round of Camembert cheese, all for shipment to Paris. Now, near the ruins of the Butter Hall, in air that likely reeked of spoiled dairy, someone found something that struck a terrible blow: a stone head wearing the traditional peaked bonnet of a Norman dairymaid. Everyone knew whose head it was, and they placed it near her body, which somehow still stood upright under the fallen hunk of debris that had decapitated her. It sat next to her headless form for several days, one more grim sight in a place of doorways that opened onto nothing and roofless walls that looked like the last, broken teeth the Americans had forgotten to kick in. Until someone stole it.

IN PEACETIME, NORMANDY is bucolic, even jolly—the Friar Tuck of French regions. Its low, rolling green hills are divided neatly into *bocage*—the characteristic hedge and tree-topped berms that separate one cow-dappled pasture from the next. Scattered among them are medieval, half-timbered manor houses that seem improbably like the setting of Disney's *Beauty and the Beast*; you can't help but expect them all to be filled with buxom maids ready to serve up tankards of hard cider. Contributing to this somewhat tipsy air are the apple orchards along with the hand-lettered signs for Calvados which plaster the roadsides. I once followed one up a jouncing country lane into the court-yard of an old farm where the doorbell was an actual bell with a pull chain. A wee farmwife answered and, after insisting I try several samples—my protests about having to drive left her unmoved—sold me two bottles of the dangerously good-tasting apple brandy. Back home, friends later pronounced it the best thing they'd ever drunk. Judging by the faintly accusatory tone of the thank-you e-mails I received the following morning, their appreciation came on a little too strong, and dissipated once they awoke.

Next to the cider and brandy, there's all the dairy. Not only is Normandy the land of Camembert, but it's one of the few French regions to also hold AOCs for butter and cream. In the village of Livarot, they even hold a speed-eating contest every August to see who can eat the most Livarot cheese in the least amount of time; the winner is accorded the title of *le plus gros mangeur*—"The Fattest Eater."

Driving through the fat hills of Normandy, it can be hard to imagine the violence that has surged and resurged through the region's history in bloody imitation of the waves that lap its long coast. But Normans can't seem to get away from conflict—not even when it comes to their cheese. I was headed toward that coast and the dairy cooperative of Isigny Sainte-Mère, one of the factions in a battle that began in the summer of 2007. That was when Isigny Sainte-Mère, along with the dairy conglomerate Lactalis (owner of two Camembert labels) decided to start making their Camemberts with treated milk.

Since the AOC for Camembert de Normandie specifies that the cheese must be made with raw milk, the change meant they could no longer use appellation seals on their labels. This was no small matter, as French-made, raw-milk Camembert already accounted for a tiny percentage of all Camembert on the market, and 90 percent of that tiny percentage was produced by Isigny and the Lactalis-owned firms. In effect, the two companies' decision to stop making Camembert *au lait cru* took the cheese from endangered to virtually extinct overnight. As if this were not bad enough, Isigny Sainte-Mère and Lactalis then went to the French government with a heretical request. They wanted the AOC rules modified so they could go back to displaying the coveted appellation seal on their cheeses, even though those cheeses were no longer made using raw milk.

A low, keening cry of outrage sounded across the verdant lands. A Comité de Défense du Véritable Camembert—or True Camembert Defense Committee—sprang into existence; a petition to save the cheese circulated. The Association Fromages de Terroirs, those makers of promotional calendars juxtaposing nearly naked women and traditional French cheeses, came out swinging. Articles abounded; documentaries with titles such as *La guerre du camembert* and *Nos terroirs, sont-ils foutus?*—*Our Terroirs, Are They Screwed?*—ran on French television. Chief among them was *The Assassinated Cheeses*. In the film, Légasse and Svensson's first stop is Camembert; they pause at the entrance to the village so Légasse can snap the inevitable photo of the black-lettered "Camembert" sign.

And the hue spread outward, to lovers of French cheese worldwide. Speaking to the *New York Times,* American cheese expert Steven Jenkins, while defending the quality of the Lactalis-produced, non-raw-milk Camembert his store carried, nevertheless mourned what would be lost if the big conglomerates got their way. "This is a slippery slope that's getting more slippery all the time," he told the *Times.* "Eventually everything's going to taste the same—all because of profit." In that same article the sole remaining *fermier* producer of Camembert, François Durand, also protested: "To not know a real raw-milk Camembert—what a loss that would be. The variety, the diversity, the flavor of the cheese—the very heritage of our country—will disappear."

In very short order, it was war: The Camembert War. And though a cheese war might seem to verge on the ridiculous even for the French, we must realize that Camembert, even more so than other French cheeses, is not merely food. Almost all the *fromages* of France lead a twinned existence: they are cheeses, yet they are also dreams; the dream the French countryside would dream of itself if such dreams were possible, the proof that what gives France her glory and strength is alive and well. Camembert, however, is *the* dream of *the* French cheese, a *fromage* so closely linked with Frenchness in the minds of people everywhere that just the name "Camembert" evokes visions of berets and fleurs-de-lys.

To French soldiers stuck in the moldering trenches of World War I, the simple act of eating Camembert with cheap red wine was a way to connect with the Divine; a makeshift communion ceremony in which the cheese stood in for the wafer, says sociologist and Camembert historian Pierre Boisard. "It had the same circular shape," he writes, "the same white color." Such devotion helps explain why people in the destroyed town of Vimoutiers might go around nabbing the stone head of a dairymaid, even though you would suppose they might have had better uses for their time. Because, in moments of uncertainty and conflict, who better to receive your prayers than Marie Harel, patron saint of Camembert cheese.

HAREL'S STORY BEGINS, as they so often do, on a dark and stormy night. Or at least this is how it begins in *La fabuleuse histoire du Camembert*, a children's book penned by Gérard Roger, president of the Camembert Defense Committee and owner of a small Camembert museum in Vimoutiers (where a model of Harel's statue, head intact, greets visitors just inside the door). It's October 1791, two years after the storming of the Bastille, and a priest runs through rain-streaked groves of oak trees in the Norman countryside. He spies the lit windows of a manor house. A young woman answers his knock. The priest explains he's been running since dawn, trying to escape soldiers who want him to renounce his vows to the Church and swear loyalty to the new Republic. The woman, Marie Harel, gives him food and offers him a place to sleep, telling him he's at Beaumoncel manor. The priest stays on and, over the next few months, presumably blends in at Beaumoncel as well as any man with a tonsure can. Then, one day, while watching Marie fill her molds with fresh cow's-milk curd, he decides to reward her for saving his life. People in his home region of Brie, he tells her, make cheese in a similar way, only in Brie they dry the curds. Little marks of astonishment surround the picture of Marie's bonneted head in the book as she says, "Dry them?" The priest explains how to drain the curd, salt it, and age it in a well-ventilated room. Marie wonders if it will work. "You can only try," the priest says. Not long after offering his cheesemaking tip, he leaves Beaumoncel, never to be seen or heard from again.

Marie takes the priest's advice, which proves transformative. Her plain curds take on the mature, velvety richness of a real Camembert. But not only does Marie make the cheese, her daughter, also named Marie Harel, does too. The younger Marie goes on to marry an enterprising young man named Thomas

Paynel, who sells the cheese in larger and larger towns, spreading its fame. Together the younger Marie Harel and her husband have five children, all of whom found dairies so they can make more cheese. As the generations expanded, the Harel and Paynel descendants jealously guarded their exact recipe, passing it from mother to daughter. In time the family becomes, in the words of Pierre Boisard, a "Camembert dynasty"—a phrase that always makes me want to picture a montage of Joan Collins in her bathtub full of bubbles interspersed with images of Norman cows. The description is accurate nonetheless. Camembert made the Harel descendants very rich.

Still, even with such phenomenal success, Camembert remained a largely regional cheese until the mid-nineteenth century, when the railroads then twining from Paris like so many iron vines arrived in Normandy. Seemingly overnight, the vast Parisian market was a mere six hours away, instead of three days by stagecoach. Demand grew among residents of the capital (it's said) when one of the Harel/Paynel sons somehow wrangled an audience with Napoleon III. Upon being presented with a Camembert, the emperor immediately ordered a supply of the cheese for his palace in Paris, thus making it even more famous. All of this led many more would-be cheesemakers to try their luck with Camembert, each using a slightly different recipe. Many of these new *fromagers* were not above luring experienced—usually female—cheesemakers into the nearest apple orchard or haystack, in what would become a long-standing tradition of cheese espionage. (Picture the rosy-cheeked lass with a bit of straw stuck to an exposed thigh being asked between furtive caresses how long she rennets her curd. Picture her blinking at her lover in consternation.)

Apparently such tactics worked. Not only did Camembert makers within Normandy multiply, but by the early twentieth century, makers outside the region had also sprouted like field clover. The new makers were eager for a share of the market; they were not all scrupulous, however, about how they obtained it. One of the things that makes Camembert taste so good is its high fat content. The text on French cheese labels that states, for example, "40% *matières grasses*"—"40% fat"—originally had nothing to do with helping people watch their cholesterol. Instead, it let consumers know they were getting all the luscious fat content for which they'd paid. Some of the new Camembert dairies went so far as to use skim milk to make skinny, inferior cheeses they could sell fast and cheap. Not only were they underselling reputable firms, but cheesemakers in Normandy felt that the entire Camembert name was diminished.

In 1909 the Norman makers banded together to create the Syndicat des Fabricants du Véritable Camembert de Normandie. Their aim was to protect Norman Camembert. This they did by promoting it far and wide. One of their more successful schemes involved sending Camemberts to soldiers in the trenches during World War I. Though the syndicate may have been ostensibly moved by patriotism, the larger hope was that the troops would go home wanting more of the same. The soldiers did develop a taste for the cheese, only it turned out they didn't care overmuch whether their Camembert was made in Normandy. This, in fact, was too often the prevailing attitude of the French at that time—an attitude that persists to this day among many *supermarché* shoppers—and the syndicate next tried to persuade the French government to grant them exclusive rights to the name "Camembert." Year after year their pleas went unheard. In desperation, the syndicate sued a dairy cooperative for counterfeiting, and in January of 1926 an appellate court handed down its ruling. Unlike other French cheeses that had been made in the same place for millennia—such as Roquefort, which you will recall received the first AOC granted to a cheese the previous year—Camembert was too new and its production had spread too far and wide. Normandy, the court felt, had no exclusive claim to the name. The cheese had become French, and it now belonged to all French people. This meant that anyone who wanted to—including all the scurrilous makers outside Normandy, and even around the world—could call their cheese "Camembert."

AND PRETTY MUCH anyone did. This was the situation in March of 1926 when Dr. Joseph Knirim, an American, strode into Vimoutiers one fine spring day. Dapper in a check suit and carrying a cardboard suitcase, he would have walked from the railway station into the center of town where, perhaps drawn by the familiar sight of medicine-filled vials, he stopped at the door to the local pharmacy.

Inside he found Vimoutier's pharmacist, Auguste Gavin, who also served as deputy mayor, and Gavin's friend. The two were up to their brushy mustaches in planning that year's Easter fair. Knirim baffled both men by explaining, in broken French, that he intended to visit the nowhere town of Camembert. But there could be no mistake after the doctor pulled a letter of introduction in French from his suitcase: "Savarin, the famous epicure," the letter read, "said that it was more worthwhile to invent a new dish than to discover a new star. How much more precious, therefore, must be the invention of a new dish of equal benefit to both the sick and to those who enjoy good health." The doctor, it seemed, had cured both himself and his patients of chronic stomach ailments by prescribing a strict regimen of Camembert and pilsner beer. Now Knirim had come to Normandy to pay his respects to Marie Harel at the monument in her honor. Since there was no such monument, and no one had ever even heard of Marie Harel, Gavin and his friend bundled the doctor off to a hotel. The pharmacist then left for a conference with the mayor, and it didn't take the two of them long to decide that the whole Marie Harel thing could be a bigger boon to tourism than even colored eggs.

In a matter of days Harel's remains were located, and Dr. Joseph Knirim placed a wreath of gilt laurel leaves, decorated with miniature versions of the American and French flags, on the tomb. In good French style, the people of Vimoutiers held a lavish lunch for the doctor before he left town. Over dessert, he conveyed his fervent wish that a statue be erected to honor the inventor of Camembert and made a first contribution toward a monument fund. Then he continued on his merry way to Plzeň in Czechoslovakia, where he intended to pay homage to that town's life-giving beer. Two years later Vimoutiers unveiled the unfortunate stone dairymaid who would eventually lose her head, clothed in a dress, apron, and the traditional Norman large conical white hat. Behind her was a stone frieze inscribed with the words "*À Marie Harel, Créatrice du Fromage de Camembert.*" A former French president attended the event. Dr. Knirim did not. Evidently even cheese and beer can stave off death for only so long; in the aftermath of his tribute tour, the obliging American doctor had passed away.

It's all rather too convenient, of course. Boisard, whose thorough history of the cheese is tellingly titled *Camembert: A National Myth,* confesses, "I myself have wondered whether [the Knirim story] was not invented out of whole cloth by the Norman cheesemakers to promote their products." Boisard does allow the possibility that Knirim (who was a real American doctor) might have learned about Marie Harel (who was a real Camembert maker in Normandy) through various articles published in the United States, but beyond that, matters become rather fuzzy. By Boisard's count, there are at least twenty versions of the Knirim tale, each melding verifiable fact with legend. Still, setting aside the story's flaws—and it has quite a few—the aura Marie Harel gave Norman Camembert was unmistakably powerful. So much so that on at least one occasion a peasant couple was seen kneeling to pray at the foot of her statue. Other regions and even other countries might produce the cheese, but they could not claim to have birthed Marie Harel. She was just what the Normans had been looking for: a heroine, a cheese goddess, a Camembert rock star.

OR PERHAPS HAREL'S appeal lies less in her sanctified aura than in her guise as farmwife. Boisard notes the symbolism of the passing of knowledge from the priest to Harel—the cheese moving from God to the secular realm. Harel might be saintly, but she's also a peasant woman: earthy and potentially alluring. Adam Gopnik reminds us that dinner is often a prelude to sex (at least for the dating couple), and for French diners, obviously, the final course before the evening's activities get under way is none other than cheese. (It's also possible that serving *fromage* after the meal is a bit of homeopathic wisdom stuck in the culture: the calcium and phosphate in cheese work to counteract acid in the mouth. It may also be a matter of practicality—if you take your cheese out of the fridge with the other ingredients for dinner, it has arrived at the optimal temperature for tasting by the end of the meal. Then again, these aims need not be mutually exclusive:

eat your cheese at the end of the meal and you get a good-tasting *fromage* that leaves you clean-toothed and ready for copulation.)

And Camembert, which ripens from the outside in, until it reaches what Boisard calls the "ultimate oozing stage," is a sexier cheese than most. Boisard (clearly no Camembert prude) describes the oozing moment as the point at which the ripened *pâte* "evokes other emissions, both male and female, menstrual or spermatic, according to one's tastes and fantasies." If connecting ripe Camembert to bodily fluids doesn't strike you as either appetizing or arousing, Boisard claims it has the opposite effect on the repressed: "Here, men who are unable to speak simply and openly about their sexuality allow their imaginations full rein."

Menstrual and spermatic emissions aside, just trying to pick a good Camembert does involve a certain raciness. "Who knows what Marie Harel was doing with that priest, after all?" my friend Philippe Lherminier asked, smiling slightly as he tested an unsuspecting rind with his thumb. We were standing in the aisle of an Intermarché grocery store in the Norman town of L'Aigle, where Philippe had taken me for a tutoring session on the art of choosing a Camembert. In the cases before us were stacks and stacks of different brands. Philippe had begun by pulling off lids left and right so I could see the ridge of *croûte* at the outer edge of the wrapping; when ripe, it's a golden to reddish brown. Smell is important, too—Pierre Androuët offers dire warnings against cheeses that smell like ammonia. "If you can detect it, the Camembert is *passé*—'gone.' It will be sharp," he says.

But the most important thing to do with your Camembert before buying is to touch it. "Palpation," Androuët admonishes. "All soft cheeses should be felt gently throughout their mass. Begin at the edges and work toward the center." So Philippe and I stood there fingering the cheeses, testing for just the right amount of give that meant the cheese would be soft but not runny. (It's possible to eat them chalky, but I don't recommend it.) According to Colette—who was so well known for her love of cheese that she has her own entry in the *Larousse des fromages*— he ought to have just left the entire matter to me: "A woman knows how to choose a cheese better than a man," said Colette. "Feeling the *croûte,* judging the elasticity of the *pâte,* divining a *fromage* is a little bit like alchemy."

We'd driven to the grocery store from Philippe's house. Perhaps the reason Normandy always reminds me of a Disney movie is that it's the only place in the world where I know someone who actually lives in a château. Located forty-five minutes from Camembert, Philippe's smallish—well, small for a castle—sixteenth-century abode, Fontenil, has actual towers, banks of windows crisscrossed by diamond-shaped panes of leaded glass, an echoing main hall flanked by hearths large enough to roast an entire barnyard worth of animals, and fifteen bedrooms. When I pulled up before his ornately carved front door, I'd found Philippe sitting on the steps in a salmon-colored T-shirt and camouflage pants, tying his shoelaces as he waited. He's a tall man, barrel-chested, with a bulbous nose, white hair, and a white beard. When we left to go to the grocery store, he threw on an ancient leather bomber jacket that made him look like a French Commando Father Christmas, then settled behind the wheel of a rattletrap car. Before his retirement, he worked as a geneticist—a cow geneticist. Even better, his grandmother had made Camembert. If there were an informed opinion to be had on how Camembert and science and technology evolved together, I figured Philippe could supply it.

"*Un chèvre ordinaire,*" Philippe had mused in the afterglow of a lovely lunch of paella as he picked up the log of "ordinary goat cheese" on the table beside him. "Everyone thinks it's the little old *grand-mères* who make the best cheese, but it's the technicians." He contemplated the *chèvre*. "Taupe Boojay," he said, reading the "Top Budget" brand off the label. "They take something and give it to a team of engineers and tell them: 'You have one year to figure out the composition of this product and replicate it.' Once they've done that, they say: 'Okay, now figure how to make it at half the price.' And," he said, sounding sardonic and admiring at once, "they do!"

THIS, OF COURSE, is what traditionalists fault Isigny Sainte-Mère for doing: subjecting Camembert to laboratory analysis, then coming up with a way to produce something that tastes like the traditional product while still meeting the demands of the modern market. The morning before my visit with Philippe, I'd pulled into Isigny Sainte-Mère's parking lot, leaving my car near a flank of hangar-like corrugated metal buildings and a dozen or so enormous stainless-steel milk tanks. Among producers of traditional French cheese, Isigny is big, employing some 500 workers and transforming approximately 53 million gallons of milk per year into cheese, butter, powdered milk, and the like. But alongside Lactalis, its erstwhile partner in the raw-milk debacle, Isigny Sainte-Mère is a blip: With 54,000 employees and 3.83 billion gallons of milk transformed every year, Lactalis is the world's largest dairy conglomerate, third in the world. It's the leading producer of cheese not only in France, but also in Italy; its iconic offering, launched in the 1960s, is the ubiquitous mass-market Président line. In other words, Lactalis is the many-tentacled monster that keeps lovers of traditional *fromage* awake at night.

Most observers of the Camembert war focused on Lactalis spokesman Luc Morelon, a vaguely toadlike, jowly Frenchman who likes to insist that raw milk has nothing to do with the taste of Camembert. Isigny Sainte-Mère, on the other hand, didn't seem to get much attention other than to be mentioned in the same breath with Lactalis. That made me curious. As it turns out, Isigny is no Lactalis: its corporate headquarters is sizable but not huge, housed in a utilitarian cement-and-glass office building that's perhaps a third the size of your average Walmart. Still, no one could accuse Isigny Sainte-Mère of lacking corporate flair; the receptionist presided over a desk in a cavernous lobby, and when commercial director Luc Lesénécal appeared, he showed me to a shiny conference room where a laptop, projector, and pull-down screen awaited. He was joined by Jérôme Goulard, in charge of marketing. Lesénécal looked fiftyish, while Goulard could not have been older than thirty-five. Both were nattily dressed in slacks and ties.

Lesénécal, who'd called me at home in the States to arrange our meeting, took the lead, while Goulard chimed in here and there for what proved to be the most corporate of any morning I spent on the cheese trail in France. I must admit to some bemusement as I was treated to a PowerPoint presentation focused on export percentages, total sale revenues, ISO certifications, etc., complete with color-coded graphs. The Isigny Sainte-Mère co-op, they explained, prides itself on innovation. For instance, it had recently invested in a generator fueled with salvaged wood, which both saves money and limits CO_2 emissions. Another of its innovations had to do with Mimolette, the orange cheese that owes its tough rind to cheese mites. Jérôme explained that after its salespeople noticed that shopkeepers tended to push Isigny's Mimolette aside—a well-aged round is so difficult to cut that it once sent American cheese man Max McCalman to the emergency room for stitches—the co-op began providing sellers with laser cutters.

As the PowerPoint presentation came to a merciful end, I asked why the company had decided to stop producing raw-milk Camemberts, and why it felt justified in asking that the

AOC rules be changed. "Look," Lesénécal began, "you have four techniques. You have *lait cru*; you have pasteurized milk, where the milk is heated to a high temperature for a short amount of time; you have thermalized milk, where the milk is heated to a lower temperature for a longer amount of time; and fourth, you have microfiltered milk." He paused. "Have you been at a farm to see the milking?" I said I had. "Well, back when cows were milked by hand, using a milk jug and bucket, the top of the jug was covered with a piece of cloth, which was the filter. Quite simply, the micro-filtration is a filtration, only it takes place here." With micro-filtration—in which the milk is passed through a series of tubes containing high-tech porcelain filters that remove 99.9 percent of all microorganisms—the milk is never heated. The idea that this was the same as straining milk through a scrap of linen was questionable, but Luc continued with his rationale: "Compared with pasteurization or thermalization, you don't destroy the consistency of the milk; you don't destroy the proteins or the lipids," he said. In other words, the milk, though filtered, could be considered intact. "Microfiltered milk has exactly the same characteristics as raw milk," Luc insisted, "except that the bad bacteria are removed."

From the conference room, we prepared to visit the factory so I could see Isigny's Camembert making in action. As Goulard peeled off for other duties, I signed a waiver promising I was not a carrier of the bubonic plague or any such disease, and suited up in a cloudy white bonnet, a white coat, and a pair of

knee-high white rubber boots, an ensemble that had me looking like a deranged deli worker. "I feel very pretty in this outfit," I commented to Luc as we crossed the road to the factory.
Once inside, I was asked to disinfect my hands and then to step
through trays of disinfectant. On the other side of this gauntlet
was, without question, the largest *fromagerie* I'd set (a very clean)
foot in: long, narrow rooms filled with stainless-steel machinery and thousands of white plastic molds moving by conveyor
belt. Luc showed me the pipes for the micro-filtration. After the
milk has been filtered, Isigny Sainte-Mère adds back what he
described as *nos souches sauvages*—"our natural wild strains" of
bacteria—cultivated, he said, on their *terroir*. He went to great
pains to emphasize that these were not chemical additives, but
natural ones (albeit cultured in a lab).

In one misty room—sections of the Camembert factory
steamed with enough heat and moisture that I was likely getting a facial standing upright—we came upon another Isigny
Sainte-Mère innovation: a machine ladler. Twenty shiny ladles
lowered simultaneously into a vat of curd. Each captured a glob,
then rose, and shifted to deposit the curd into molds waiting on
the conveyor. The process satisfies another key rule for AOC
Camembert, which states that Camembert de Normandie must
be *moulé à la louche*.

Originally, of course, *moulé à la louche* meant "hand-ladled
into the molds." Camembert, in fact, is a particularly demand-
ing and fickle cheese. This was especially true in its early days,
when makers relied more heavily on natural lactic fermentation

than on rennet to produce curds. Those early curds not only took some five or six hours to form, but were also tricky to manipulate: if molded too soon, they fell apart; if molded too late, they clumped and wouldn't drain properly. And not only must Camembert be ladled, but it has to be ladled in five successive ladlefuls spaced precisely forty-five minutes apart. Imagine the Norman dairymaid working in a small *fromagerie,* a vat of curdled milk at her side, surrounded by dozens, and possibly hundreds, of round Camembert molds. She toils in a quiet frenzy, starting with her ladle at one edge of the vat and working in a spiral pattern as she lifts the curd to nestle a dollop into each mold. The first round completed, she moves on to the second, then the third, the fourth, the fifth. She sweats with exertion, feels the dampness rising from the wet floor, which must be kept very clean, the strain in her legs from standing for hours at a time. The work was hot, heavy, and long.

And that was just the start. Once molded, the cheese must be turned and then salted, a matter so delicate that good salters were highly sought after and commanded high wages. Superior aging required special drying facilities, called *hâloirs,* which were outfitted with ventilation systems that required skillful and continuous manipulation to ensure the correct humidity throughout the twenty- to twenty-five-day *hâlage* process. From the *hâloir,* unfinished Camemberts went to the *caves* to be aged some more. Throughout these stages the cheeses also had to be regularly turned.

The demands of Camembert making meant there was much

to be gained by moving rapidly toward proto-industrial production. The operations of Marie Harel's own grandchildren were far from quaint farm outfits. By the mid-1850s, the two largest dairies, each owned by a Paynel brother, made 40,000 Camemberts per year, while another brother, Cyrille, produced some 30,000 annually. By 1879, Cyrille alone churned out 150,000 rounds. In order to sustain this level of output, Camembert makers in Normandy began outsourcing milk production, a big shift from traditional ways. Producers then embraced other technical improvements, electrifying their operations and making use of steam-powered equipment.

When it came to the cheese itself, scientists from the Pasteur Institute were called upon to lend their expertise, especially with various strains of mold. Camembert is a *croûte fleurie*—a "flowered-rind cheese"—meaning that its rind develops as mold blooms on its surface. In the beginning, that mold came in rather alarming shades of blue-gray and gray-green, thanks to *Penicillium camemberti,* a native Norman mold strain. Harel herself had to work at persuading customers to buy her cheese in spite of this off-putting appearance. So the scientists got to work isolating *Penicillium candidum,* the happy spores that make a Camembert as white as the bosom of a pure Norman maid.

If Pierre Boisard is to be believed, the new mold changed more than simply the color. Camembert, he says, "became less sharp, losing its peasant bite and thereby enlarging its circle of admirers." These new and improved rounds were shipped to Paris in the newly invented Camembert box, which meant they arrived in the capital looking as white and perfect as they'd been when they left Normandy. No more hick, barnyard-y cheese, this.

Then along came the Americans, blasting Marie Harel's head from her neck—a fitting metaphor for how the Second World War would affect not only Camembert, but all French cheeses. If the original war to end all wars had devastating consequences for Justine Carbonié and others like her living in rural France, the changes it brought were nothing compared with those precipitated by World War II. In a few very isolated areas—think high in the mountains, at the end of a long dirt path—cheesemaking would continue without much change. But by and large, the Second World War marks a turning point in the history of almost every traditional French cheese. There's the period before the war and then there's the *après guerre*.

Postwar France entered a phase of rapid expansion. For the hungry population pulling itself from the rubble, the first priority was to ensure that bellies and pockets were filled. Camembert production charged ahead, turning into a true industrial powerhouse. (Brie, the cousin cheese of Camembert, was similarly influential on the opposite side of the Parisian basin. But in the end, Brie, a much larger cheese, couldn't compete with Camembert's conveniently family-size rounds.) Producers who had been reticent before the war about fully utilizing scientific advances now regularly called in technicians to help control outbreaks of *P. camemberti*. Nor did they hesitate to take drastic measures—

often the only way to rid a factory of unwanted mold strains was to tear the old building down and build a new one.

Pasteurization, too, saw a sharp increase in popularity. Though the technique had been in use in France since the late nineteenth century, it became widespread only in the decades following the war. And Camembert makers in particular discovered that the technique offered a host of benefits. For one thing, it allowed them to skip the ladling step altogether. Heating milk coagulated its proteins, meaning that the resulting curd drained differently. Such curd required cutting, after which it could be poured, rather than ladled, into molds. Though the process changed the texture of the finished cheese, it also cut labor drastically. In addition, pasteurization protected makers against accusations of endangering public health.

The trouble with unpasteurized milk is that it's volatile—alive, as it were. On a small farm, where the milking of one herd is carefully managed, the risk of contamination is almost nil. But start combining the milk of several farms, holding it in tanks, and transporting it over long distances (as began to happen in earnest both in France and the United States with the advent of railroads), and the chances of outbreaks of listeriosis, tuberculosis, and other scary stuff ending in "osis" mounts exponentially. Such outbreaks can occur with any sort of milk, though historically speaking, most of the risky milk came from cows—most goat and sheep farms simply didn't produce enough milk for shipping. And soft cow's-milk cheeses such as Camembert present a particular challenge. In a hard cheese, the number of disease-causing bacteria decreases as the cheese ages. That's why it's legal to import into the United States raw-milk cheeses aged over sixty days—and why importing a raw-milk Camembert, which is aged three to four weeks at the most, is illegal.

Between 1998 and 2005, the CDC recorded thirty-nine outbreaks in the United States linked to the consumption of raw milk or raw-milk cheeses, resulting in some 831 illnesses, 66 hospitalizations, and one death. Raw-milk proponents brush aside such concerns and seek the stuff out anyway: in Europe, you can even find *lait cru* sold in vending machines. They cite studies that have linked raw milk and raw-milk products to health benefits, such as reduced allergies. Fans on our side of the Atlantic, meanwhile, have been known to resort to some impressive skulking for a raw-milk fix (the liquid kind), even though its sale is either restricted or banned in most states. The *New York Times,* for instance, has divulged that clandestine drop-off sites exist across the Big Apple, all part of a raw-milk black market.

Fans also note that treating milk does not necessarily guarantee security. Any dairy product can become contaminated if improperly handled, and serious incidents have arisen involving cheeses made with supposedly "safe" milk. This was once the case with the type of cheese Chris and I smuggled home from Paris. In the late 1980s, Swiss makers of Mont d'Or decided to begin thermalizing their milk as a preventive measure. A virulent outbreak of listeriosis followed, and perhaps unsurprisingly,

French-made raw-milk cheeses took the initial blame for the rash of fatalities. Death by cheese is rare, but it does happen, and with both types of cheese—just as food poisoning outbreaks sometimes occur with tomatoes or hamburger or lettuce. One scientist I spoke with, Eric Beuvier of the Institut National de la Recherche Agronomique (INRA), was relatively untroubled by the potential for danger posed by a *fromage au lait cru*: "Getting in your car and driving to work every morning is riskier than eating a raw-milk cheese."

Still, in many consumers' minds, raw-milk products are particularly unsafe. (Or maybe too sexy, if Boisard is to be believed—he reasons that those who have it in for soft raw-milk cheeses just can't take all that eroticism threatening to bust its rind. "Hidden Puritanism is thus reentering through the back door," he writes. "Now that it has been banished from the bedroom, the moral order is trying to get at us at the dining table.") Whatever the case may be, U.S. FDA regulations aren't exactly crafted for nuance, and consequently raw-milk AOC Camemberts are shut out of the vast American market, a market where consumers increasingly recognize appellation labels as a sign of quality. Even in France, companies worry about appearing negligent. Isigny Sainte-Mère points to a 2005 incident in which four young French children became ill after eating raw-milk Camembert; some of them, Luc Lesénécal said, would likely be affected for life.

As the tour wound down, Lesénécal and I had a small *dé-*

gustation. He cut me a slice of ripe Camembert made with microfiltered milk. At three and a half weeks, it was all blowsy permissiveness, the very image of epicurean dissipation. As I took a bite, he declared, "You're tasting *le meilleur Camembert du monde.*"

HAD FRANCIS ROUCHAUD of the True Camembert Defense Committee been in the room, I doubt he would have agreed I was setting my teeth to the world's best Camembert. Rouchaud, who is retired from the milk industry, dedicated the better part of a year to creating a sprawling website for the committee, the home page of which featured a picture of a Camembert superimposed with the words *Je ne veux pas être otage*—"I don't want to be a hostage." As far as Rouchaud was concerned, milk must be completely untreated if it is to carry that thing that defines real Camembert. "If you want the true cheese, you have to go back to the farm," he told me, insisting upon using a slow, precise English, even though I was answering in French. I got the impression he wanted to be very clear.

The farm he was referring to was that of François Durand— the only farm there is when it comes to Camembert making. Visiting that farm, however, proved to be something of a challenge, as Durand did not respond to my repeated phone calls or messages. I had finally been forced to ask my friend Philippe to intervene, aware that sometimes a native can get further than some pesky American *journaliste* on a cell phone. "I don't have time for her," Durand told Philippe. But Philippe, being French, managed to talk Durand into letting me tag along with a busload of tourists by simply repeating, "But yes, yes, but you see, my idea is can't she just join onto the group" (accompanied by swooping arm gestures that Durand could not possibly see over the phone each and every time Philippe repeated "just join onto the group") until the poor man agreed.

The following morning, I took my leave of Philippe and headed toward Camembert and the Durands' farm, stopping at Vimoutiers on the way. After the war, a group of American Camembert makers who heard of the inadvertent desecration of Marie Harel's statue took up a fund for a replacement. As a result, the plaque below Harel's feet now reads, in English: "This Statue Is Offered by 400 Men and Women Making Cheese in Van Wert Ohio USA with the Cooperation of the Committee on Aid to Vimoutiers." If the first Marie Harel statue wasn't exactly pretty, looking rather dour instead, its replacement is a splendid example of the dull heights attainable by civic art. Her features are blunt and inelegant, and her peaked Norman peasant hat makes her look like a very unattractive oversize salt cellar. It was hard to imagine anyone praying at her feet.

The morning was waning by the time I arrived in Vimoutiers, but at one end of the square a handful of market stalls sold wares to stragglers. I meandered over and, to my surprise, found a cheese labeled "Camembert fermier." It claimed to be *au lait cru* and *moulé a la louche*. It was not, however, made inside the AOC zone for Camembert de Normandie. Intrigued, I bought one for €3.40. That was ten centimes less than the Durand cheeses on offer at a nearby stand. Like the counterfeits of the old days, it was apparently trying to undercut sales of "true" Norman Camembert.

Just before reaching La Héronnière, the farm of the Durands, I passed through Camembert, a postage-stamp of a place consisting mostly of a town hall, a tourist office featuring an overhang in the shape of a Camembert box and a machine that allows you to create your own Camembert label, a church, and a small Camembert museum owned by Lactalis. As I pulled into the farm, a crowd of silver-haired and clearly vigorous French men and women piled from a bus: French retirees of a certain age pursue gastronomical touring the same way that Americans go on RV tours of our national park system, attended by similar feelings of stirring nationalism. We all trooped into the visitor area, a long rectangular room dominated by a table covered in a green-and-white-check cloth. Pictures dotting the walls showed François Durand stooped over rows of molds, ladling curd by hand. He was a vastly skinny man with a shock of dark hair and glasses that made him look like a French-cheese version of Harry Potter.

His wife, Nadia, was petite and a tad plump in a pleasant way, with a mop of tousled dark hair knotted at her nape. She wore a dark green apron over a black T-shirt, high heels, and a pair of the uber-stylish eyeglasses all vision-impaired French women seem to be issued at birth. Her manner was forthright and sure as she launched into a history of the farm. Her husband's father had kept dairy cows but didn't make cheese, so François had to go outside the family to learn his trade. Finding an artisanal maker of Camembert had proven difficult. In fact, François had only one option: Daniel Courtonne, then the last *fermier* maker of Camembert in existence. After Courtonne retired, Durand's skinny shoulders were left to bear the Camembert mantle alone. When Patrick Rance visited the Durand operation in the mid-1980s, he reported that the Durands made a thousand Camemberts a week from the milk of twenty-eight cows. Nadia told us that the farm now had a production of four hundred cheeses per day, made from the milk of sixty or so cows, including some native Normandes. (When writer Michael Steinberger visited the operation in the company of Rouchaud and other members of the True Camembert Defense Committee, the men assured him that even though François doesn't milk those cows by hand—which would, of course, be the very best thing he could do—they were willing to be magnanimous about this one small deficiency.)

As small producers, the Durands face a number of difficulties. Bringing the *fromagerie* up to current EU sanitation norms cost €300,000 alone. Nadia noted the recent defection of Isigny Sainte-Mère and Lactalis from the AOC, pointing to a poster on one wall that identified the ten producers formerly making AOC Camembert. Someone had drawn *X*s in thick black marker over

Isigny Sainte-Mère and the two Camembert brands owned by Lactalis. She named each of the six small producers still making AOC Camembert, "the only ones *au lait cru,* the only natural ones," and showed portions of a film of François making his cheese. He didn't dare stop for even ten minutes while filling his molds, she said, or he would throw his entire timing off. I marveled along with everyone else at the mind-boggling labor.

Using a sample mold, ladle, and small metal disk, Nadia demonstrated how the newly molded cheeses are weighted and left to drain overnight. By the following morning, when they're unmolded, "it's already a *fromage,*" she said. "But it's like feta: hard, dry, rubbery. And yellow. Very yellow," thanks to the carotene found in grasses. In the past, the color was a good way to judge quality—everyone's butter and cream went yellow in the lush summer months, but white in winter. "Now they use colorants all over the place, so you don't know what's natural or not." After salting, the *Penicillium candidum* is added. "It's a mold we buy," Nadia said, "because the natural one, the *camemberti,* is gray-blue. And if you saw a gray-blue Camembert, you'd think it was going bad. Pasteur isolated the white mold, so we sprinkle the white one." As she talked, I wondered how substituting one strain of mold for another for the sake of coloring the *croûte* was technically that different from adding a dye for the sake of coloring the *pâte.* Nadia, for her part, seemed blithely unaware of any possible contradiction as she invited the group to come see some of the lab-developed white mold in action.

As the group walked to the back of the *fromagerie,* I caught a glimpse of François through a window, wrapping cheeses with an almost feverish speed. After we'd gazed through more windows at dozens of Camemberts, some still draining, some bright yellow with youth, others already growing misty coats of mold, we all filed back into the reception room. François appeared behind the counter at one end of the room, ready to help Nadia with the clot of people already gathering before the cash register. Eyeing him, I couldn't help but remember that he'd not really wanted me there. I also noticed that the man looked even gaunter in person, as though he could really use a good fattening up on his own cheese. I fought the tide to where he stood by the counter.

"*Bonjour,*" he greeted me.

"*Bonjour,*" I said, explaining that I was the American writer. He bobbed his head, smiling politely. I returned his smile. What do you say to the one person in the world stubborn enough to keep on making Camembert by hand? I turned and left him and his wife in peace.

THAT EVENING I set out the Camemberts I'd collected while traveling through Normandy in preparation for tasting. There was an Isigny Sainte-Mère Super Médaillon made with microfiltered milk that Lesénécal had given me before I left the co-op, the counterfeit raw-milk *fermier* Camembert from the market in Vimoutiers, and a cheese I'd gotten from what had once been Philippe's grandmother's store. She'd made four hundred cheeses a day before selling her business in 1927, the same year people up in Vimoutiers were in the thick of making plans for the original Marie Harel statue. On the morning of my departure, Philippe had taken me to see her old place, which had been turned into a minuscule gourmet food shop, an *épicerie fine*. Inside, several Camemberts sat in a glass case. The label for one pictured a woman in traditional Norman costume, a yellow crock of curd and metal *fromage* molds on a wooden table before her. In her left hand she held a ladle, while on either side of her bonneted head scrolled the words "Marie Harel." When I asked the woman behind the counter who had made that particular Camembert, she'd promptly replied, "Marie Harel." I bought one immediately.

The counterfeit proved too young to judge: firm and positively chalky. I put the Isigny Sainte-Mère up against the Marie Harel (closer inspection had revealed it to be made by the Laiterie de Saint-Hilaire de Briouze, one of the handful of small producers still using raw milk). Both were perfectly ripe. Both tasted the way a good Camembert ought: salty and eggy, slightly mushroomy and truffle-y, a distillation of the jolly fatness of Normandy. The big difference was in the texture. The Marie Harel was creamy, but also just a hair rubbery. The Isigny Sainte-Mère, on the other hand, dissolved on the tongue in what I want to describe in all seriousness as dulcet lusciousness. It was the *croûte* that really sealed it, with a visible difference in the two rinds: in the Marie Harel, the contrast between *pâte* and *croûte* was almost nonexistent, while the Isigny Sainte-Mère rind floated on the *pâte* and was almost crunchy in a quite wonderful way. The Isigny Sainte-Mère, the one made with microfiltered milk, was simply a better cheese.

It was, in fact, better than any Camembert I've tasted before or since, including the very tasty bite of François Durand's cheese I'd sampled before leaving his farm. This, of course, is a large part of the trouble. It isn't that the people at Isigny can't make a good Camembert with treated milk. It's that they make a predictably good Camembert. Such versions of Camembert made with treated milk can be so good, in fact, that even informed French consumers can have trouble figuring out precisely what they're buying. My friend Patricia, a native of Tours, once brought home a Camembert packaged in a deliberately plain wooden box with the words *Le Rustique* burnt onto the lid. The cheese also carried the words *fabriqué en Normandie,* and was wrapped in a little red-and-white-check kerchief. She and I had been sitting in her kitchen discussing the Camembert brouhaha. "That's a good one, though," Patricia said, jutting her chin toward the box I held in my hands. "It's *au lait cru.*" I flipped it over and read aloud: "*au lait pasteurisé,*" at which point Patricia, who prides herself on her knowledge of French food products, sniffed and went back to the dishes she'd been washing.

Very few things separate a Camembert de Normandie from its imitators around the world: the milk must come from Normandy, the cheese has to be ladled (whether by hand or by machine), and the milk must be raw. I agree that keeping that milk raw is likely the best way to ensure an authentic link between cheese and *terroir*—and to retain the lovely inconsistency of the real thing. "I like to be surprised by the taste," Eric Beuvier of INRA told me. "That's why I like raw-milk cheeses." For me, too, part of the appeal of a cheese *au lait cru* is that I never know exactly what I'm going to get. It's a new experience every time.

That said, those who argue that requiring the use of raw milk will preserve the history of Camembert might want to give that history another look. Rouchaud, of the True Camembert Defense Committee, was unequivocal in his condemnation of Isigny Sainte-Mère and Lactalis: both were simply out for profit; both had no respect for tradition. But to condemn Camembert makers for wanting to change the recipe because they're "all about profit" is to condemn them for being traditional. No one in the history of Camembert has ever labored to make the cheese simply for the sheer joy of hard work.

Not only that, but how do you even begin to say what the real traditional Camembert is? By 1850 the cheese was already fairly industrialized, meaning it was a farmhouse cheese for fewer than 60 years. For the last 160 or so years (almost three-quarters of its history) most Camembert production has been either firmly industrial or heading there. Along the way, the Camembert recipe has been interpreted and changed numerous times, with lots of help from scientists and technicians. The AOC for Camembert, in fact, wasn't granted until the 1980s, by which time the *véritable* had been dropped from the old name of Véritable Camembert de Normandie. This was because no one could say what exactly "true" meant when it came to Camembert.

Perverse as it might seem, a move to treated milk is actually more in keeping with tradition than an insistence on raw milk. But the Camembert War, like all wars, has little to do with logic. Equally paradoxical is the idea that the AOC is the perfect tool to stave off the standardization of a cheese and protect small makers. But maybe we can't expect reason when dealing with a cheese constructed of myth and romance and legend. It's no doubt fitting that Léon-Paul Fargue, the poet who once dubbed Camembert *les pieds de Dieu*—"the feet of God"—was a surrealist, versed in the hidden meanings of our dreams.

The French government ultimately turned down the requested change to the AOC rules, essentially accepting the argument that science and technology don't mix well with tradition. Back in the Middle Ages, the soft cheeses of Normandy (forerunners of Camembert relatives Livarot and Pont l'Évêque) were called Angelots, after a coin depicting an angel defeating a dragon. You might say that the True Camembert Defense Committee, like the medieval angel, has slain the beast of industry, and not long after the Camembert war ended, the Isigny Sainte-Mère cooperative introduced a new cheese called Camembert Excellence. The rounds are marked very clearly, in large, white script: *"Au Lait Cru."* Their capitulation is understandable. After all, everyone wants to be on the side of the hero. The trouble is, in some parts of France, it was not the angel who would save traditional cheese. In some parts of France, it was the dragon who would come to the rescue.

HIGH ON A HILL

~~~~~~~~~~

"Many's the long night I've dreamed of cheese—
toasted, mostly."

—ROBERT LOUIS STEVENSON

J ean François Villiod stood in the narrow gap between the
wall of his cheesemaking shed and the rim of a hot-tub-
size copper kettle containing the last of the day's milk from his
herd of eighty-odd cows. Two corners of a linen cheesemaking
cloth were knotted behind his neck like a giant bib. The other
side of the cloth he held open with a band of thin, flexible metal
that would allow him to swoop that edge of the fabric down and
along the kettle's curvature. He clenched the middle of the cloth
in his teeth. The average round of Beaufort uses the curds from
more than a hundred gallons of milk and can weigh nearly 150

pounds, or as much as a small Saint Bernard. If he's really good, the cheesemaker can capture those curds in one scoop of linen, leaving just the whey. This was what Villiod, arms and teeth full of cloth, was after as he balanced his pelvis on the copper rim, then walked his Wellington-shod feet up the wall behind him. His torso tilted forward on the fulcrum of the kettle as he went, allowing him to extend his reach across its full circumference. Body nearly horizontal, he balanced on the edge of the vat, teetering on the brink of cheese.

"*L'instant de vérité*," he joked—"the moment of truth"—to the little crowd gathered for the evening cheesemaking: my friend Sarah, the woman Villiod was seeing, a few of his children, a few of hers. Chilly Alpine air streamed through the open doorway behind us, making me wish I'd brought more than a light sweater. Earlier, Villiod had encouraged us to put our hands into the tub. Somewhat wary of the steaming surface, Sarah and I had exchanged looks, then plunged our hands in up to our wrists along with the kids. As soon as we did, I decided I was never taking my hands out. I would spend the rest of my life frolicking in warm curds and whey. Villiod had stuck his hands in the vat, too, though his aim was more purposeful. Knowing when the curds are ready is part of the Beaufort maker's art, and Villiod scrunched a handful of grainy, pale white curd, testing its resistance, using his fingers and palm to divine the moment when what had been just separated cow's milk was ready to become one of the most marvelous cheeses of France. He handed round bits of curd for us to try. "It doesn't taste a thing like Beaufort," I said, chewing industriously. The curds, in fact, tasted like nothing at all—even more tasteless than the plastic-y cheese curds I'd squeaked my teeth into as a kid in Wisconsin. Villiod gave me a look, as if to say, "Well what did you expect?" The curds, after all, were not Beaufort—not yet.

I'D FIRST TASTED Beaufort several weeks earlier, when I'd gotten it the way most French people get their *fromage*: from a good cheesemonger in an open-air market. The *marché* was in Annecy, a lace doily of a city half an hour or so south of Geneva by car, on the edge of the impossibly picturesque French Alps. (At one point, while Sarah and I were hiking in the surrounding mountains, I gave into an irresistible urge to spin, arms out, and sing, "The hills are alive! With the soooound of muuusic . . ." Sarah looked at me. "That's the fastest anyone I've brought into the Alps has done that," she said in a tone that could have dried dishes. "With songs they have sung," I pressed on, prancing down the path "for a thooousand years!" I almost expected to see children dressed in playsuits made from curtains. Sarah heaved a sigh and trudged after me.)

As I drifted about the medieval portion of Annecy, I believe the only words to come out of my mouth were "*C'est charmant.*" The crooked stucco buildings lining its cobblestone streets were charming, the canals that threaded its center were charming, the vines and pink geraniums that sprang from every nook were charming. And around the city, which is attached to the cleanest lake in Europe—it has a special filtration system—the slopes are crammed with ski lifts and charming wood-beamed chalets.

I was there amid all of that loveliness because of Sarah, a super-slim brunette who looks French, teaches French, and speaks French like a native, but who grew up in California. A few months earlier she'd said to me over dinner, "If you're going to be in France this summer, you could come stay with me." People who know me should really never make those sorts of offers. Before long, I was camped out on the floor of the studio apartment she'd rented for the season—one room with a stove, sink, and mini-*frigo* shoehorned into a nook in one wall. A closet-like bathroom hid behind, appropriately enough, a mirrored closet door. Paneled in violently cheerful blond wood, the place boasted a fold-out futon and a set of dining room chairs, each with a single heart carved through the back. Sarah had dubbed it the Heidi Hut.

The Heidi Hut's most charming feature, however, was its location smack-dab in the middle of Annecy, which happens to be smack-dab in one of the most famous cheesemaking *départements* of France: the Haute Savoie. Cheese is at the center of life here. Take the local specialty, *tartiflette*. My first night in Annecy, Sarah (who'd said something along the lines of "Yeah, dude, *cheese!*" when I first told her about my French *fromage* mission), turned a deaf ear to my protests about jet lag and dragged me to the Pig Restaurant. Not that it was actually named the Pig Restaurant—that was what Sarah and a friend of hers from Geneva called it. A giant pink pig statuette greeted us at the entrance; various other pigs festooned niches and walls, and the woman's toilet appeared to have been fairly invaded by representations of pigs. The whole thing reminded me of the few years I lived in barbeque-crazy Kansas City, Missouri, and couldn't seem to find an eatery that wasn't all about swine.

We dined on *tartiflette*: potatoes, butter, onions, some type of meat (usually cubed bacon), and a rind-washed cheese known as Reblochon, all mixed together and stuck in an oven until it turns golden brown. It's tough to overstate the importance of this marriage of cheese and tuber in the Savoyard mind. Nearly every restaurant in Annecy serves its version, and the city's astronomy association, Tycho Brahe, even holds a "Startiflette" party every summer in the peaks above the city: Reblochon, potatoes, and telescopes all raised to the heavens. The one we sampled at the Pig Restaurant reminded me a lot of the scalloped potatoes and ham my German grandmother used to make, though when I voiced this sacrilege, Sarah shook her head, temporarily rendered speechless.

The cheese, of course, is the essential ingredient, and I was to hear the Reblochon origin story so frequently during my visit that I came away convinced every Savoie native must have it memorized from infancy. Instead of uttering *Maman* or *Papa* as his first word, the little Alpine child just launches into "Reblochon was invented in the thirteenth century . . ." and continues on about how taxes on peasants used to be calculated according to the milk produced by a herd in one day, so the landlord would visit the farm periodically in order to monitor the yield. The wily Savoyard farmer, however, stopped the *traite* before the cow was completely dry. Once the medieval IRS departed, he did a second milking, which produced a smaller but richer quantity of milk, which he used to make cheese for the family. In the area patois, *reblocher* meant "to pinch the udder a second time," so the petit theft became known as *la rebloche,* and the cheese Reblochon—a cheese born of tax evasion.

BUT REBLOCHON IS only one sort of *fromage* to be found in Annecy. The city so overflows with cheese generally that even the local Monoprix (France's answer to Target) carries more than fifty artisanal cheeses, many of them with AOCs or labeled *fermier,* not to mention a smattering of foreign offerings such as cheddar and Manchego. And this was just in the deli counters at the front of the store; there were several more aisles of cheese back in the dairy section.

The very best place to see cheese, however, is at the *marché*. One Sunday morning, while Sarah was off visiting friends, I ventured out onto the cobblestone streets under a sky that periodically erupted into rain. The door to the Heidi Hut gave directly onto the main drag of medieval Annecy, where the *marché* takes place three times a week. On market day, merchants extract myriad impromptu storefronts from undersize vans packed tightly along the narrow corridor. Seeing the *marché* appear from the vans was like watching one of those gags in which clowns and more clowns keep popping out of a car: one moment the world is ordinary, and the next it's filled with color and an almost silly sense of giddiness. Where before there was only gray stone and shops selling T-shirts, suddenly there were boxes stuffed with salad greens and cartons of cherries, strawberries, and currants. There were olives, a dozen different sorts swimming in brine; silvery anchovies dripping in oil; and dozens of varieties of *saucisson,* the dried sausages that made American summer sausages seem like wan pretenders. (Even at their most undignified—such as the bulging round sausages I saw that had been packaged in pink cardboard cut to resemble frilly ladies' underpants—*saucissons* reign supreme.) There were baskets of artichokes and girolle mushrooms; piles of green and red sweet peppers; stacks of cucumbers, radishes, leeks, carrots; potatoes with dirt still caking their pale skins; and eggs complete with chicken fluff. There was a stubble-cheeked man selling a couple of rabbits he likely shot in a nearby field, and a worn nubbin of a French country *grand-mère* crouched in a corner on a stool gently peddling her own honey. And then there were the cheeses.

Many of them sat naked, stacked in wooden cartons and piled one on top of the other behind makeshift glass barriers. In most regions, the *marché* is the place to find smaller cheesemakers, those who still "make the markets," as they say in French—setting up a stall in one village on Monday, in another on Wednesday, and in still another on Friday. In Annecy, one man had a folding table draped in a red oilcloth and set with three trays of little patty-like cheeses and a hand-lettered sign that read, *"Fromage de chèvre fermier."* The sign was illustrated with a hand-drawn goat's head, presumably for foreign tourists who might not recognize either a goat cheese or the word for it. Other stands had cases protecting *faisselles* of *fromage frais* and hunks of butter wrapped in paper.

Many of the cheeses littering the stands were *tommes,* some sliced open to reveal centers of creamy white. A *tomme* is any medium-size round disk of hard, pressed cheese with a tough rind that can be dark or light, brown or gray, or flecked with little starbursts of orange mold. It's a basic cheese form in France, one produced nearly everywhere, with any kind of milk, though the Savoie is famous for cow's-milk *tomme,* the best known of which is Tomme de Savoie. The word itself likely derives from the Greek *tomos* and the Latin *tomus,* meaning "part" or "piece"; *tommes,* at least in the Alps, were often made with the excess (or "part") of the milk left over from making other, larger cheeses.

Most impressive were those larger cheeses, hefty rounds hailing from the mountainous regions of eastern France: Comté, Abondance, Emmental—and of course Beaufort. Technically speaking, Beaufort is a *gruyère.* This is a tad confusing when one of the best-known *gruyères* is Le Gruyère. But like "cheddar," *gruyère* also describes a type of cheese, one that falls into the pressed and cooked category. The technique for making them originally came from around the town of Gruyères, in Switzerland, itself named for the *grueries*—"forests"—surrounding it. (The *grueries* were managed by an agent *gruyer,* who sold firewood to the cheesemakers and in return was paid in cheese.) Beginning in the early 1900s, a battle ensued between French and Swiss producers of *gruyère* over who had the right to use the term. In 1930 a panel of cheese experts convened in Rome to discuss the matter. They decided that both countries ought to be able to use the name jointly, and AOCs were eventually awarded for both Swiss and French Gruyère. Even so, the Swiss version continues to outcompete the French one, with the result that almost everyone considers Gruyère of the big *G* to be Swiss, and most *gruyères* in France are called something else.

To get my Beaufort, I stood in line at one busy stand where the cheese seller assiduously seesawed his long two-handled cheese knife through the round. I'd chosen him because, for whatever reason, his Beaufort seemed to glow. Maybe it was because the wedges were slightly elevated, perched atop other huge, tannish rounds. Maybe it was the rain-washed light. Maybe it was all the wine I'd had the night before. Who knows?

"How many kilos?" the man asked when it was my turn. I wasn't sure, so he angled his knife over a good-size slice and said, *"C'est bon?"*

"Yep, that's good," I said, not really caring how much I got, so long as I got some. Back at the Heidi Hut, I sat in one of the heart-back chairs before the table. I never tire of the moment when I first open a cheese: turning the paper down to reveal the *pâte,* getting the first whiff of its particular scent. A light odor of hazelnuts and yeast sifted from the folds. Then I sat before my Beaufort, just looking. The wedge was luminous. This is not hyperbole: I swear this cheese was sunlight in cheese form. I cut a finger-size piece, put it in my mouth, and understood why Brillat-Savarin called Beaufort "the prince of *gruyères.*" Not only did it smell of hazelnuts, it had their sweet-salty taste combined with the melt-in-your-mouth texture of a fine steak. Lovely, crunchy crystals—clusters of tyrosine, a type of amino acid that forms in a well-aged *fromage*—flecked the *pâte* here and there like bits of candied cheese. I swallowed another slice, closed my eyes, and sighed.

An odd fact about cheese is that it abounds in casein, a protein that breaks down in the digestive system to produce an opioid called casomorphin. Just what, if anything, casomorphins do to the human body is controversial. They've been linked to an array of diseases as well as to a number of health benefits, though hard evidence seems difficult to come by. According to Neal Barnard, an American doctor/author/researcher (and veganism advocate), "the most powerful [casomorphin] has about one-tenth the narcotic power of pure morphine. It's not enough to make you drive erratically, but it is enough to give a certain ad-dictive quality to these foods." All milk-based products contain this apparently dangerous substance, he warns, but it's cheese we really need to watch out for, because it's the purest, best sort of casein you can get. In the words of the good doctor, "you might call it dairy crack."

I'm willing to bet that Beaufort is up there on the casein scale, and on that day in the Heidi Hut, I became an unabashed Beaufort junkie. I knew that I could live on Beaufort alone for months at a time, that even if it killed me I'd die a happy, Beaufort death. And I knew that I had to see this cheese being birthed, warm and steaming, from its kettle.

SARAH WAS UP for the hunt. It had been clear from the start that she envisioned my journey as a sort of cheese version of Jack Kerouac's *On the Road*—she was the one who first told me about casomorphins. "Dude," she kept saying, "you have to put yourself out there—let crazy things happen. You know. Hitchhike." I had a tough time convincing her that nice girls from Wisconsin don't hitchhike, not even for cheese. A rented Renault was as close as I was getting to standing on the side of the road with my thumb out, clutching a sign that read, "Beaufort or Bust." Sarah contented herself with making a CD of wanderlust-imbued car songs, and we hit the highway with Willie Nelson blasting from the speakers as we screamed along: "On the road again! I just can't wait to get on the road again . . ."

We'd picked up an *itinéraire des fromages*—a cheese map that can be found in a number of French regions—from a local agricultural office. The map was colorful and nicely produced, and included the addresses of various cheese locales. Wedged between listings with actual street numbers, the directions to the Villiod place seemed especially antiquated. They went something like this: Go to the don't-blink-or-you'll-miss-it town of La Bâthie, drive in the direction of Biorges, then, after the funeral marker, follow the signs to Bellachat. The more I drove in France, the more I would come to understand that navigating the Hexagon is an art requiring instinct, blind faith in signs pointing the way to the next village, and the conviction that if you just keep moving forward it will all work out. Not only is the road-numbering system seemingly random, but it's as though cardinal directions cease to exist—there's no such thing as Highway X East or West. Nor is there much point in asking for help—anyone you stop will just tell you that wherever you're going is *tout droit, Madame*—"straight ahead."

Sarah, who's spent far more time in France than I have, knew this very well, but even she was flustered by what we had to work with. "Can't we call for better directions?" she asked, palming her cell phone.

"We could if there were a phone number," I said. After driving *tout droit* in several directions, we managed to locate La Bâthie, then nosed through it, looking for the funeral marker. "Do you think that's it?" we asked each other, passing several vaguely promising bits of rock. Finally, we spotted a weathered white cross and some stones, followed by a wooden sign inscribed with "Bellachat" and an arrow pointing the way. I turned the wheel, and we began to climb.

THERE ARE ACTUALLY three different kinds of Beaufort. There's Beaufort *d'hiver*—"winter Beaufort"—a relatively bland cheese made when cows are in the barns eating hay and feed. (I tasted some once; it was dangerously close to sliced deli Swiss.) There's Beaufort *d'été*—"summer Beaufort"—made from the milk of cows grazing high-altitude summer pasturage. And then there's Beaufort *d'alpage*. *Alpages* are the Alpine equivalent of an *estive* in Auvergne—mountain pastures where cheesemakers go with their herds during the summer months. But the Alps have historically been less isolated than Auvergne, and *alpages* at lower elevations are typically housed in cute peak-roofed *chalets d'alpage*. You can often tell which chalets house cheesemakers by the huge cowbells hanging from the eaves. Many animals are quite aware of their own bells, if Patrick Rance is to be believed. He writes that "cows have been known to be so upset when their bells crack that they give no milk for forty-eight hours." Bruised livestock feelings may sound far-fetched, but research backs up the notion that happy cows are productive cows—for example, one study found that cows that are given names turn out to be better milkers. No doubt the bells hanging from the eaves—decorative, special-occasion ones the cows wear for the short *transhumance* (usually just a few miles) up to the *alpage*—give them all sorts of warm feelings.

Below the bells, most *chalets d'alpage* have windowboxes dripping with pansies and wooden picnic tables where people sit around admiring the views and eating bread with freshly churned butter. As late as the 1950s it was common for the cheesemaker's whole family to set up shop at the *alpage* starting in early June, when the weather is crisp but not cold, and wildflowers dot the hillsides. Dad, Mom, and kids would all trot along with the cows to spend a few months at their summer abode. At night mothers tucked their children into trundle beds, where they fell asleep to the tinkle of distant cowbells. Many of these lower-elevation *alpages* are still in use today, turning out an assortment of smallish *fromages* such as Reblochon or *tomme*.

Beaufort *alpages,* however, were a different matter. A few weeks after arriving at their summer digs, the little family at a relatively low-elevation Reblochon *alpage* could look out their door to see a caravan of eight or so men with rucksacks leading pack mules up the trail past their house, accompanied by a combined herd of eighty to one hundred cows. The snows had melted from the peaks, permitting them to go up—way up. Every round of Beaufort bears a label made from casein, the same protein found in milk; the labels stick to a new cheese and become part of the rind. Today a round of Beaufort can't bear the red casein square that certifies it as AOC "Beaufort Chalet d'Alpage" unless it was made at an elevation of at least 1,500 meters, or more than 4,920 feet. This altitude is more than okay by the cows, as the billions of bacteria in a cow's stomach give off so much heat as they break down plant matter that cows much prefer the cooler air at 5,000-plus feet. By late summer, the herd might range more than a mile and a half above sea level. Even in pleasant weather, there's not much going on that far up the mountains besides the growing of grass and the scudding of clouds.

Once at the *alpage,* the men settled into rough, bunkhouse-style quarters and got to work. The day began in darkness with the first milking. After that was done, the men strapped silver milk jugs to their backs and walked back to the chalet, where they cooked their curd over a wood fire. The curds were removed from the kettle using a cheesecloth tied around the ends of a thick wooden log; the setup required a team of two men, one on each end, to heave the newborn cheese upward and out. Then there was pressing and salting and turning to be done, cows to tend, and another milking and cheesemaking in the evening. The day ended around ten. High Alpine cheesemaking made for harsh, remote summers—the "break" between cold winter months in the valleys below. It was, according to one cheery Savoyard saying, "Nine months of winter, three months of hell."

INCHING ALONG the mountainside, Sarah and I were beginning to see for ourselves why the saying painted such a grim picture.

Living in the American West, I've done my fair share of mountain driving, but never on a road that was more of a gesture at a road than a road, and never in a tiny, stubby-fronted Renault. Back in the day, cheesemakers used to transport their finished cheeses down roads like this one by placing them two at a time onto the backs of pack animals in specially built cases capable of handling the 250-plus-pound payload. We zigzagged up switchback after switchback; I blessed the manual transmission every time I downshifted for traction. Looking down at the trees that covered the slopes, I found myself thinking that if we did pitch off the crumbling pavement, at least we wouldn't fall very far.

Clearings appeared in the forest whenever we wound past chalets, several of which had signs indicating the elevation. We translated meters into feet: 2,000, 2,500. But structures dwindled rapidly as we climbed, giving way to clumps of purple harebells while the scent of chamomile drifted in the open car windows. "I counted thirty-six plant species in flower within a few square yards near the road," wrote Rance of one *alpage*. Any *fromager* will tell you that the quality of his cheese depends heavily on what the animals are eating; the flavor and aroma of flowers and herbs work their way into the milk and from there into the cheese. The sort of diversity of flora that Rance describes— and that Sarah and I were seeing and smelling—is what gives Beaufort and other mountain cheeses their richness.

An hour, a wrong turn, and some 4,500 feet later, we sat contemplating an unmarked, unpaved track that looked nearly vertical. We'd rejected it out of hand twenty minutes earlier in favor of what turned out to be a dead end.

"We can't possibly be meant to go up that," Sarah said.

"We could hike it," I said, edging the car forward. The sun was lowering in the sky, and the map said the evening cheese-making went from six until eight o'clock. We were already late. The car slipped and skidded upward. At the top was a small parking area and a picnic table clearly intended for the public. We had arrived.

Taking the muddy trail leading from the parking area, we soon came upon nine cows with glossy coats of rich chestnut. They were Tarines, one of the AOC-approved Alpine breeds. From where we stood with the cows, we caught a glimpse of one of the rudest chalets I'd yet seen anywhere in the Alps, plopped on a slight rise above us. Two minutes later, Sarah and I stood knocking at its plank door. Up close, the place was a tumble of multihued stucco, exposed stone, thick plastic siding, and out-size roof beams topped by corrugated metal. There wasn't a single pansy-stuffed pot in sight. A collection of green plastic lawn chairs with a matching green table that seemed meant for tastings stood nearby. A nearly new "Itinéraires des Fromages" sign hung from the peak of one gable, where it looked rather like the hood ornament of a Cadillac welded onto a rusted-out pickup.

No one answered our knock; the place seemed deserted. Up the trail, a long, low barn sat tucked into a slope. As we looked toward it, a pickup towing a dented spherical milk tank detached itself from the distance and headed our way. A young guy, baseball cap pulled low, sat at the wheel. As the truck drew near, we asked about the cheesemaking, and the man said, "Sure, you can go on up." We plodded along the rise to the barn. Yellow pails, milk jugs, and a pair of green rubber milking boots lay before an open door. Poking our noses inside, we glimpsed the two copper-lined cauldrons.

Stepping gingerly onto a floor of white tiles still slick from a recent cleaning, we found ourselves in a little room walled off from the barn. A guy who looked to be in his twenties turned to greet us. A necklace of braided leather brushed the collar of a white T-shirt under his full-length rubber smock, and a couple of days' worth of stubble lent his face a pleasantly fuzzy air. Short curls of dark hair lay damply on his forehead above a pair of winsome brown eyes. His name was Etienne—he was the summer cheesemaker—and he looked more than a little startled at our sudden appearance. Once he learned we'd turned up to watch the cheesemaking, however, he became clearly delighted. He whisked about, washing away the muddy tracks we'd made on his clean floor before leading us to a hose by the door so we could wash the bottoms of our shoes.

Inside the room and opposite the cheesemaking kettles stood a wooden tabletop, rather like a big door set on its side with a grooved track around its perimeter. Behind this were three tall metal beams with arms jutting from the top of each, like hangman's gallows. Viselike handles of the sort used to screw down hatches on a ship extended downward from each arm. A round of cheese still in its wooden mold sat beneath one of these contraptions; the vise was screwed down tight over it, pressing. Next to it sat another round, naked on a rectangle of linen, looking like an outsize lemon cake. "Here, you can touch it," Etienne said, and we put our fingers on its springy top, the surface still bearing the puckered imprint of the linen.

The Bellachat *alpage* produces three rounds of Beaufort a day, Etienne explained, and these were the two from the morning. Over the summer, they'll produce some 360 rounds in total. We turned toward the agitating kettle, underneath which glowed the blue flames of a propane burner. Etienne explained that he was at the "cooking" stage, heating the developing curd to at least 130°F. The heating expels more whey, helping to create a cheese that is dry enough to last throughout the long aging process. Etienne dipped a hand into the steaming kettle and came up with a mass of curd. It needed another forty minutes or so, he said.

The sides of a Beaufort have a signature convex curve. Two ropes cinched the circumference of the cheese that was being pressed in its mold. I had read that the tension of the rope made the curve, but Etienne shook his head; the ropes just hold the mold together. He pulled a mold from a nearby hook to show us the inside, which matched the exact curve of a Beaufort. Made of ash, the molds are called *cercles à Beaufort*—"Beaufort circles"— and they're an artisanal trade themselves: only one company makes them. Slits make the circle flexible enough to fit around the cheese. Etienne stretched the one in his hands nearly flat to demonstrate, and it yielded like one of those slinky snakes made of wood. Finally, he handed us a battered binder while he busied himself rinsing cheesecloth. Inside the binder were examples of the casein labels for *alpage* Beaufort and a brief highlight of the cheese's AOC rules. Beaufort Chalet d'Alpage must be made from the milk of one herd, we read, both morning and evening, in the traditional manner.

It was a manner that almost hadn't made it through the postwar upheaval of the 1950s and '60s. As the country modernized, anybody with options began to think maybe they could do better than spending summers stuck in the middle of nowhere, especially in the days before *alpages* had generators and indoor plumbing. Women in particular began to rebel against this way of life. Girls were becoming more educated, and cheesemakers were hard pressed to find a lass willing to marry them when doing so meant committing to what was viewed as a life of rural servitude. The French countryside was, in fact, at the beginning of a long emptying-out. At the end of the war, some 36 percent of the population worked in agriculture; over the next four decades that figure fell to 7 percent. Such difficulties, combined with an increasingly competitive cheese market, meant that a Savoyard countryman could make a better living sweeping chimneys in Paris than he could making cheese.

With the cheesemakers disappearing, the very *alpages* were

going away, too. Legions of grazing cows had long helped to keep the pastures open; now trees began to sprout (a change in the landscape that also disrupted entire populations of birds and butterflies that had depended on the open habitat for centuries). Ski resorts began to fill the mountains with lifts, while new hydroelectric projects inundated pastures. After the construction of four dams for one such project, fifteen *alpages* where Beaufort had been made slipped silently underwater. By the 1960s, Beaufort production had fallen to a scant five hundred tons a year. The cheese was in very real danger of going extinct.

Enter Maxime Viallet, a small, neat-looking cheesemaker—in one photograph he's dapper in a suit and vest, tie expertly knotted, white-gray hair swept back from a broad forehead, black shoes shining—who would come to be regarded as a local hero. Viallet's parents had been *alpagistes,* and he was a tireless Beaufort supporter. (When Pope John Paul II visited Annecy in 1986, Viallet was on hand to present the pontiff with an entire wheel of Beaufort.) Viallet and some of the other producers who had stubbornly clung to making Beaufort could see that their way of life was rapidly disappearing. They could also see that if they, and the cheese along with them, were to survive, they were going to have to organize and make some strategic decisions.

The answers sound familiar today, but at the time, as Viallet has said, the cheesemakers were regarded as "originals." Rather than racing after the rest of the country to industrialize on a massive scale, they would concentrate on small-scale production with a few twists. The most significant of these was the introduction of the very thing that the producers of *The Assassinated Cheeses* later deemed too industrial to be shown as part of making Salers, *le top* of artisan cheese: the *machine à traire*.

As early as the 1950s, makers had been trying to ease the burden of hours of laborious hand-milking—yet another big reason so many were abandoning high Alpine cheesemaking—by hauling rudimentary milking machines into the mountains on the backs of mules. But it was difficult to get such equipment into remote locations, and if changes tended to happen slowly in rural France, the impulse to resist innovation was especially pronounced in remote mountain areas. It wasn't until the 1970s that the *machine à traire* really began to make a difference. Beaufort makers spent the next thirty or so years refining the machines, and today the ones used in the Alps are far larger and more elaborate than those of Auvergne. A modern Alpine *machine à traire* is a long, trucklike affair, complete with walk-in milking stanchions for the cows, that follows the herds as they migrate. In other words, Beaufort makers used technology—in a very targeted and savvy way—to save their traditional cheese.

SARAH AND I walked back toward the house with Etienne. On clear days, he told us, Mont Blanc was visible to the east, and when the clouds shifted, we felt we could almost see the massive peak. I asked how many tourists came for the cheesemaking.

"Oh, two or three sometimes," Etienne said, though at times as many as ten. "How many Americans?" I asked, and he grinned. "You're the first ones I've seen," he said, though he added that there were occasionally a few Québécois thrown in with the French. I asked what he did when he wasn't making cheese, and he said he kept busy feeding the pigs, washing things up, and turning the cheeses. When I asked if he liked living up in the mountains all summer, he appeared genuinely nonplussed, as though he'd never before taken the time to consider whether he liked it. "Well, yeah, sure, it's nice up here," he said, and added that it was a good way to spend the months in between his other job, as a lift operator at a ski resort.

As we approached the chalet, a man popped his head and bare torso out of a nearby door, hair wet from a recent washing. This was Jean François Villiod, owner of the *alpage*. The look on his face said he wasn't entirely certain what to make of his cheesemaker returning from the cheesemaking shed with two women in tow. He glanced down at his naked chest, then back up at us. Etienne said we were Americans who'd come to see the cheesemaking. "*Non,*" he replied in a tone that made it clear he thought Etienne was putting him on. As Villiod ducked back in to get dressed, Etienne smiled broadly, clearly enjoying the joke. Villiod reappeared in jeans, a T-shirt, and a woolen vest. At possibly forty-five, he was slim and wiry, bespectacled, and very trim. His movements were economical, those of a man who'd performed the same tasks over and over and knew what he was about. At the moment, he was about to take over the cheesemaking. Etienne had the night off because, as he explained with a blush, it was his twenty-eighth birthday. "Now you have to kiss me, you know," he said, and Sarah and I took turns standing on tiptoe to place kisses on each of his sweetly furry cheeks before he toddled off for his night on the town.

Half an hour later Villiod stood scrunching his cheese curds and hoisting his linen *toile* in preparation for his ascent partway up the wall. He gripped the band of thin, flexible metal that held open the edge of the fabric. One of his sons—the guy from the pickup truck we'd spoken to earlier—stood with us, ribbing his father about whether he would get all the curds: "Etienne never leaves any behind." Steam rose from the kettle, and Villiod wriggled forward on the lip. As he swooped the edge of the cloth down and along the kettle's curvature, the fabric-covered band disappeared under the surface of the whey, then reappeared on the opposite side of the kettle.

"Did he get them all?" one of the kids asked. It seemed he had. He slid the metal from the cloth, reached for the corners of the linen that were tied behind his neck, and knotted all four corners together. He looped the knotted cloth over a large metal hook connected to a rope wound through a pulley overhead—a decided improvement over the two-man log-hoisting team from the old days—then muscled the curds up and out of the kettle by pulling on the rope. Whey gushed as he swung the pulley, with its bundle of suspended curd, along a metal I-beam attached to the ceiling that led from the kettles to the waiting mold. Once he had his bundle centered over the mold, he released the rope and plopped it in. Then he squished the curds down with his hands, sending whey streaming everywhere. He would turn the new round after about five hours, and again five hours later, he said. It was nearly 8:30 at night. It occurred to me that cheese-making may explain some of the craziness often attributed to mountain people: They're all sleep-deprived.

Outside the cheese shed, a fine rain had begun to fall. I thought of the steep road down in the growing cold and wet. We followed Villiod to his cheesemaking *cave*. Earlier in the evening, Etienne had shown us the stone-lined room, perhaps fifteen by twenty feet, that lay half buried in the slope underneath the chalet's living quarters. A bare bulb hanging from the ceiling illuminated a strip of fly-pocked tape and twenty-seven rounds of Beaufort arranged on wooden shelves along the back wall. Three more linen-shrouded young cheeses occupied a table in the middle, while another two bobbed in a saltwater-filled tub. From one of the mature rounds, Villiod cut a slice that weighed nearly a pound and a half, which he sold to us for ten euros, absolutely dirt cheap for Beaufort d'Alpage. We thanked him and then we were racing down the path to the car, noses red, clutching our cheese.

The gray scree slopes across the deep draw off to our left were dotted with patches of snow, and over them lay low clouds, their underbellies tinted pewter in the dying light. In the aching distances between ridgelines, the cheesemaking shed and chalet were the only structures visible. As Villiod had disappeared into the chalet, I thought I heard the sound of a television coming from inside, and pictured the kids grouped around the screen, maybe watching *À la Recherche de la Nouvelle Star*—the French version of *American Idol*. The little family would sleep that night perched above their scant thirty-two cheeses. Even with television, it was a lonely place.

By bringing the *machine à traire* to the mountains, the Beaufort makers of the postwar years saved the pastures, which saved the quality of the milk, and in turn made it possible for cheesemaking to continue in high-elevation *alpages* such as Villiod's operation. Sarah and I could not have been more grateful for this as I eased the Renault down the mountainside and she clawed her way into the Beaufort, using her bare hands to tear off pieces, which we stuffed into our mouths. Even so, these days *alpages* are only part of the equation—and a small part at that. Where once the cheese was made almost exclusively at the higher elevations, today very little Beaufort—less than 6 percent—is considered *alpage*. A few decades ago there were thirty or so high-elevation *alpages* still making Beaufort; today there are only a dozen. In order to truly move Beaufort into the modern world, an entirely different way of doing things would be necessary. An entirely different—and much bigger—way.

BIG FRUIT

~~~~~~~~~~~~

"A poet's hope: to be, like some valley cheese, local,
but prized elsewhere."

—W. H. AUDEN

As late as the mid-nineteenth century, the Jura Mountains—heavily wooded scarps that spread from southern Alsace to northwestern Savoie before spilling over into Switzerland—still housed sorcerers. Everyone knew that turning milk into cheese required the involvement of other realms, and cheesemakers used their powers in various ways. They could locate lost items and predict the future. They could simultaneously milk their entire herd while they sat around cleaning their teeth with splinters of wood. And they never bothered with locking up their chalets, since anyone who violated the sanctity of the *fromagerie* soon paid the price: One such thief who tried to steal a cheese, or so the story goes, found himself trapped in place by an invisible force. He remained stuck on the threshold for two days, a heavy round balanced on his shoulders.

Such tales are easier to believe when you're actually in the Jura, wending through thickets of moss-trunked spruces so dense you can be five minutes from a town yet feel as if you will be forever lost. It's the sort of place where you can imagine pixies roaming and wood sprites playing tricks. The sort of place where you can open a door in a hillside and find some one hundred thousand giant disks of golden *fromage*.

ORIGINALLY, OF COURSE, getting into that hillside wouldn't have been so easy. Fort Lucotte de Saint Antoine is an underground fortress, just one of more than 150 forts constructed along France's eastern frontier in the aftermath of the Franco-Prussian War. Some 600 masons, 600 stonecutters, and 3,000 soldiers labored to construct the massive subterranean structure, complete with an encircling ditch and drawbridge and capable of garrisoning 420 men. Not long after the fort's completion in 1882, alas, the invention of a new type of shell capable of ripping through that much-labored-over masonry rendered the site obsolete. And so it lay abandoned for nearly a hundred years, left to the skitterings of forest creatures and the dares of children from the nearby village of Saint Antoine, who used its flat, sod-covered roof as a playing field. Until a day in 1966 when cheese *affineur* Marcel Petite must have stood not far from a pair of crumbling guardhouses, contemplating the fort's façade: a wall of rough-cut stones and a doorway topped by a wide, unadorned frieze built into the side of a grassy mound.

The head *caviste* at St. Antoine, in charge of the fifteen or so people who now work there year-round, is Claude Querry—a lean, dark-haired man so continuously in motion that every photo I snapped of him turned out blurry. He explained Petite's instant infatuation with the site: "From his first visit, he fell in love—it was *un coup de foudre extraordinaire*." What Petite fell for, once he passed through the doorway, was the even, chill humidity of the place, how the lovely dankness filled room after room after room. It was exactly what he'd been looking for.

When we hear the word *cave* (pronounced in all its French glory, so that the vowel sounds like the *a* in *lava*), most of us picture an actual cave—a natural hollow of rock, or at least a cellar, perhaps with vaulted ceilings. But most *caves* in France today are not caves at all—they're temperature- and humidity-controlled rooms, often aboveground. Not only are natural caves scarce, they're often inconveniently far from roads and require extensive outfitting if you're to have lights or running water or any hope of meeting sanitary regulations. Finding ones that lend themselves to cheese aging can be a challenge.

One can imagine the excitement Petite must have felt, then, as he walked around in the pitch black of St. Antoine, no doubt swinging a flashlight on the walls of the underground space, already complete with water and ventilation systems. And then there was the size of it: more than three hundred thousand square feet. This mattered because not only did Petite want to age a lot of cheese, he wanted to age a lot of really big cheeses, specifically the Jurassien specialty known as Comté. Like Beaufort, Comté is a *gruyère,* though rounds of Comté are flatter and bigger than a Beaufort, have a convex rather than a concave rind, and average eighty-five or so pounds next to Beaufort's one hundred or so. A round of Comté is called a *meule*—"millstone"—and in his first year at St. Antoine, Petite aged approximately 2,500 *meules.* Over the next forty or so years, the Petite family business would renovate vast portions of the fort, outfitting the former bunk rooms, vaulted stone passageways, and roomy central court with nearly two and a half miles of wooden shelving—shelves that now hold some 100,000 wheels of Comté. If you laid those 100,000 rounds out end to end, you could tiptoe across the *fromage* for some thirty-four miles, or the length of more than 600 football fields. It's a lot of really big cheese.

Cowbells jangled melodiously over a sound system as Claude led the way deeper into the fort. Though the fort is a serious working cheese *cave*, its renown means that each year it gets more and more visitors, and as a result it's well turned out for tourism, with informative placards and spotlights strategically placed to illuminate the stone walls. It was a fitting environment for Claude, who was just as spiffy as the facility he ran. Like most *af-*

fineurs, he was keenly interested in all sorts of cheese. Just the day before, he'd been in Auvergne to watch Salers being made. And when I mentioned that I'd recently visited a nearby *fromagerie* to watch the production of Mont d'Or, he quickly offered to find me a more artisanal operation. I nodded, but didn't explain that I'd been content to watch as a couple of women deftly girded rounds in spruce strips (smiling and waving when they saw me watching through the upstairs observation window) without having to worry about anyone pressing a sample on me.

Mont d'Or, you may recall, is the odiferous wonder Chris and I had dragged home from the trip that started me on my quest years earlier. We had spent most of the holiday season abroad, straggling in the door on Christmas Eve to a cheerless house. The following day, we escaped to a friend's Christmas potluck, bearing our stinky prize. The lady of the house took one whiff of the booty, which we explained with some pride had come directly from France, and whisked it into the depths of her refrigerator. We never saw it again. In the end the story became funny, but even so, we both felt almost cheated. By then, I'd read that Vacherin Mont d'Or was produced only during the cold months in the mountains near the border of France and Switzerland— the perfect Christmas *fromage.* To make up for this disappointment, I'd decided that the only place I was tasting a Mont d'Or was in Paris, with Chris, on Christmas.

Authentic enough or no, the Mont d'Or *fromagerie* was quaint—positively Lilliputian, really—in contrast to St. An-

toine. Given the capacity of just the Petite *fromageries* alone—
they have a second, more modern facility that holds 80,000
rounds—it's no surprise that Comté making generally is not just
big business, it's huge. At 45,000 tons per year, Comté has the
largest production of any AOC cheese, far outstripping the an-
nual production for the next two *fromages* on the list: Cantal at
19,000 tons, and Camembert, at 12,500. An estimated 40 percent of French households eat Comté. Yet in spite of turning out
ton after ton of cheese, Comté making—and aging—remains
artisanal.

Claude stopped before one of the interior courts. On any
given day, most visitors see a mere twenty thousand of the tens
of thousands of rounds in the *caves*. Claude, however, apparently
felt that number insufficient, and proposed that we tour some of
the sections not open to the public. As he went off to get me a
white coat, I stood with Séverine Vitte, a tiny, breakable-looking
blonde with shoulder-length curls from the Office de Tourisme in
nearby Métabief, who had decided to tag along for the tour. As
she looked on, smiling slightly, I stood with my head tilted back,
staring upward at the towering spruce shelves filled with amber
meules. They call Fort St. Antoine the Comté "cathedral." Here
was the nave. The cheeses went up thirty high and stretched
away so far that I lost count. In one of the aisles was one of the
fort's seven robots. Robots, of course, are up there with milking
machines as a top concern for many traditionalists—as one Wisconsin cheesemaker who'd imported several of them remarked,

"Robotic artisan cheesemaking is an oxymoron!"—yet they save the *affineurs* hours upon hours of manual labor. Some *cavistes* like them so much that they give them nicknames. (One used in Beaufort aging, for example, is called Robo-fort.) The cart-like machine was utilitarian in design: essentially a flat metal surface that moved up and down between two upright posts, with mechanical arms to grab the cheeses. Up and down the aisles it went with a clatter of metal and a whoosh of hydraulics as it pulled, brushed, and flipped *meules*.

"Comté has a very old tradition," Claude said after he returned with my white coat, "but it's also modern." It was impossible to keep on turning and brushing and cleaning each round by hand in a *cave* with thousands of cheeses, he explained. "What's important is that there be a knowledge there." He pointed to different racks of cheeses. "You must adapt, and these days we have machines that are good enough they can be trusted with such work. When you buy a piece of furniture," he continued, "it might be a work of art in spite of the fact that it was made with electrical saws or other power tools. If the principle of construction is the same and the quality of the wood is respected, it goes together the same way; it's still mortar and tendon, still traditional. So what," he said with some vehemence, "if you've used a mechanical saw. So what?"

He turned to lead us along a series of corridors and stairs to an area the *cavistes* have nicknamed *la maternelle*—"the nursery school." Shelf upon shelf rose, twenty high, each filled with stacks of Comtés. Pale yellow with youth, they looked like enormous Nilla Wafers. These were the *bébés*. Until they begin to develop their adult rinds, they're coddled with daily brushing and salting—"like human babies who need to be fed," Claude said. The *cave,* too, must be closely monitored to ensure that the temperature and humidity are optimal. Claude scraped the outside of one cheese, showing Séverine and me a ruffled, pencil-shaving-like peel of rind, the *dentelle.* In a bad *cave,* the rind would either be too sticky or too dry for this "lace" to form. "We have lace," Claude continued, clearly delighted to have such girly treasures to show us two females, "and we have pearls." As the salt penetrates the interior, it draws moisture from the cheese. He pulled a *meule* partway off a shelf so we could see the droplets of water standing on its surface in tiny, perfect spheres. He tilted it, and the "pearls" skittered, intact, off the rind.

Yet Comtés do suffer some rough treatment when they first arrive. During their making, a green casein label is affixed to their rinds, but the cheeses are aged for so long at St. Antoine—up to twenty-four months—that labels can become hard to read. So the fort uses a brand to burn a sequence of numbers into their sides. (I tried telling Claude and Séverine that Americans do the same to cattle in the American West, but my explanation must have fallen short—they both just looked at me as though they couldn't possibly see how this was relevant to cheese.) Each numerical sequence tells where the cheese originated. Claude decoded a round for us: "This cheese was made on thirty-one August, 2008, in the Doubs *département,* in the village of Chapelle-d'Huin."

"In France," Séverine added, joking.

"In France, yes," Claude agreed, "and *sur terre.*"

THE PLACE ON earth he was referring to was not just any place. Earlier, on the way to the *maternelle,* we'd paused in a room where artifacts from the history of Comté making were displayed. A fake fire flickered beneath a copper cheesemaking vat shaped in the old Swiss style, with a narrow top and flared bottom, the two sections separated by a row of decorative hobnailing. An assortment of antique wooden tools hung from the walls. It looked a lot like an *alpage.* When I said as much, however, Claude said, "There is no *alpage* in Comté making."

"There's not?" I said, surprised. Just the day before, I'd been at a Retour des Alpages celebration in the nearby town of Montlebon—which is most definitely in Franche-Comté. The entire village of two thousand or so, it seemed, had turned out for a parade that featured children pulling milk jugs, a float decorated with butter molds and milk churns, and another float labeled "Traite d'une vache," with a lone, live Mont-béliarde, head down, munching placidly on a pile of hay, apparently unconcerned that it was rolling along the route on a flatbed trailer. Among these and other attractions—a marching band tooting out "Tequila," a beer cart manned by three guys wearing Holstein-spotted jumpsuits (complete with suggestive pink rubber udders), a troop of alpenhorn-carrying men who stopped every so often to sound melodious, haunting notes that made me wish for a honey-flavored Ricola cough drop—were no fewer than eight *troupeaux*. The small herds contained ten to twelve cows outfitted in full coming-down-the-mountain regalia. About each furry neck hung what were clearly dress bells; some were made of shiny, embossed metal, while others were plainer but larger, each held in place by a thick buckle of black leather decorated with floral motifs and red trim. Paper flowers bedecked the tails of some; others wore ribbons. The best adornment, though, was a diminutive fir tree about a foot and a half high, nearly covered in paper flowers, which had been attached to the top of one cow's neck buckle. The poor beast looked as though it had a giant green candelabra balanced atop its somewhat frenzied expression.

When I mentioned the event to Claude, however, he blinked and shook his head slightly. People in the Jura might have *transhumed* their cows to plateaus and the low peaks above the villages, he explained, but the Jura mountains generally don't have high-elevation *alpages,* because there are no higher elevations— the very highest mountain tops out at a little over 5,600 feet. (Compare this with Mont Blanc, which soars to over 15,000.) Instead, an entirely different system evolved, one that would prove to be influential for cheesemakers across France. In the Jura, they had what are known as *fruitières.*

The first clear references to *fruitières*—so called because cheese was the "fruit" of mountain people's labor—date to the 1300s. In the hills of the Jura, where the feudal system imposed a communal way of life, peasants lived "by the same fire, the same bread and the same pot," in the words of one old saying. Given that making just one wheel of Comté requires the raw milk of thirty or so cows—far more than the average medieval household kept—people naturally began to band together to make cheese. As we stood in the display room before the artificial flames, Claude told us how peasants would hire a cheesemaker to stay at different houses during the milk-plentiful summer months. Villagers brought their milk to the *fromager* each morning and evening.

As cheesemaking continued to grow along with the population, it became impractical to make large quantities of *fromage* on one farm or another—the danger of buildings catching fire from the huge flames needed to "cook" the cheese being a particular hazard. So villages began moving cheesemaking into one dedicated structure: the *fruitière*. Once it became possible to send cheeses by train to larger markets such as Paris, *gruyères,* with their hard rinds and long *affinage,* proved eminently suited to riding the rails—and the existence of the *fruitières* helped the makers of Comté respond quickly to increasing demand. By the late 1800s some *fruitières* were run more like factories than farms, making use of the same modern improvements others were also taking advantage of in other parts of the country, such as electricity and steam-driven equipment.

During this same period, the government of France's Third Republic conducted studies that found the country was behind its neighbors in agricultural development. In the Franche-Comté region, in fact, villages were often forced to rely on Swiss cheesemakers. French villagers would write away to arrange a contract, and a few months later a strapping young Swiss man would arrive for the summer, toting his big copper kettle on his back. This system worked well enough to get the cheese made, but the forced dependence on foreign labor didn't exactly make the French happy.

To remedy the situation, and as part of the government's goal of improving agriculture in general, officials began to promote dairy education and research. French cheesemakers were encouraged to take on local students, and the first dairy school in France was founded in the village of Mamirolle in 1888, followed soon thereafter by another at Poligny. Since both schools were in the Jura Mountains, their students tended to go to the *fruitières* upon graduating. And because scientists didn't have the resources to work on all the cheeses of France, they concentrated their efforts on a small number of *fromages*. One of these, naturally, was *gruyère*. Another was Camembert. Yet another was Roquefort. As a result, these cheeses became what food historian Claire Delfosse describes as "chosen" cheeses of France.

Fruitières, meanwhile, became ever more integral to village life. In one corner of the room where I stood with Claude before the mock cheesemaking display, I spotted a two-wheeled handcart of metal and wood, loaded with four milk jugs and looking ready to be tugged into motion. Such carts were a common sight in the early 1900s in the villages of Franche-Comté, when a stream of them would materialize in town twice a day. Some people pulled the carts by hand, while others (men, women, and sometimes children) drove horse-pulled carts, or rode bicycles, or even led the family dog rigged in a canine harness. If they didn't have a cart to haul the milk, they might arrive with jugs strapped to their backs. This flotsam of villagers and milk became known as *la coulée,* from the verb *couler*—"to flow." They were all headed to the *fruitière,* which by the 1900s could be built from standard plans for a *chalet modèle.* Former *fruitières* can still be recognized in many places by the long, narrow windows that allowed air to circulate in the milk room; the *fruitière* was often the newest and most sophisticated building in the community.

As everyone queued up, waiting to empty their jugs into a bucket that hung from a scale, farmers could check a board for town notices, while children might pop letters into the post box that was often located at the *fruitière.* Once the telephone arrived, it, too, could be found at the *fruitière,* and a provision to answer the community phone was written into cheesemakers' contracts. As each person's milk was weighed, and the total carefully tallied into a ledger, people chatted about the latest gossip. Political candidates might also show up to mingle, shaking hands and talking up villagers on the issues. The younger men and women, meanwhile, eyed one another and contemplated marriage. *La coulée* and the *fruitières* became such a fixture of Comtois village life that local poets composed songs about them.

And yet the *fruitière* was not without its darker side. As the model spread from Franche-Comté into the wider Jura and the Alps, then onto the plains, it morphed from a quaint, proto-industrial style of production into a true industrial production (as in Normandy, where ideas borrowed from the *fruitière* system hastened the decline of farmhouse Camembert). The pressures of the post–World War II period accelerated the trend. Not only were people leaving the countryside in droves, but they were increasingly shopping in the *supermarchés* springing up around the country. Grocery stores demanded a product that wouldn't spoil easily, that didn't require care once it left the factory, and that wouldn't stink up their shining, modern aisles. Many consumers preferred these cheeses to the older ones. Not only did they smell better, but they were also cleaner, with a regularity in shape and taste that was thought to be a plus. In some places, you had to be a connoisseur of the local cheesemakers in order to be assured of getting a good cheese. With these new cheeses, however, anyone could pick an acceptable round. It might not be transcendent *fromage,* but at least it wouldn't embarrass, say, a nervous young housewife when she invited the in-laws around to dinner.

Consumers also wanted mini-*fromages* that made for easier snacking. Some *fruitières* began to diversify, making *tommes* or even *crème de gruyère,* a spreadable "cheese product" made from *gruyère* and invented to feed troops during World War I. (If you've had Laughing Cow cheese, you've eaten *crème de gruyère.* La vache qui rit took off in the post–World War II period, so much so that it spawned numerous imitators with names such as La vache sérieuse, La vache heureuse, and La vache coquette.) Small, local cheeses that didn't lend themselves to industrial production didn't fit the new model, and though they might have stayed more "authentic," they began to die slow deaths of attrition. The situation was bad enough that some French observers went so far as to suggest that—given how consumer tastes were evolving—all local cheeses ought to be industrialized in the interest of saving them.

Even *gruyère,* in spite of its advantages—or perhaps because of them—became threatened. By the 1960s and '70s, Brittany had become a huge center of production for Emmental, the *gruyère* with the big eyes that we Americans think of as "Swiss" cheese. Makers of Comté found themselves competing with cheap, insipid imitations flooding the market from the far western coast of the country, the exact opposite of the cheese's original *terroir.* Like the Beaufort makers, Comté producers had to decide if they were going to attempt to compete with the industrialists, or if they were going to concentrate on quality over quantity. Happily, in Franche-Comté, the entrenched, centuries-old way of making cheese endured. Production remained comparatively small-scale, even as cheesemakers learned to take advantage of the technological advances and scientific knowledge generated by their own schools and research stations. And they began to band together for the *affinage* as well, making huge *caves* like the ones at St. Antoine possible.

It was this idea of cooperative labor, of growing a tad larger, that saved Beaufort as well. *Fruitières* had existed in the lower elevations of the Alps prior to the 1960s, but they had never before been used to make Beaufort. As Maxime Viallet and his fellow Beaufort makers set out to resuscitate their cheese, they saw they could use the model to their advantage. Today most herders with cows at the high elevations no longer make the cheese themselves. Instead, they use their machines to milk and then deposit the full jugs at designated points along mountain roads. From there, the milk goes to cheesemaking cooperatives. At the largest of these, the milk is pumped into a long row of shining copper kettles, each with a capacity of more than eight hundred gallons. The coagulating milk steams as it is agitated by electric-powered paddles, and curds are swept up from the kettles mechanically. Stacks of already molded and weighted Beauforts perch at even intervals on metal shelves suspended from the ceiling in order to allow the whey to drain onto a tiled floor. A conveyor moves the cheeses to a machine that turns them, then returns them to the shelves. Seemingly the only things the three or four humans on the floor do by hand are test the curds for readiness and push buttons.

It's not Jean François Villiod making cheese in his shed. But it's not Lactalis, either. Beaufort and Comté *fruitières* are proof that big (or at least biggish) doesn't have to equal bad, at least not if makers are committed to quality. *Affineurs* such as Marcel Petite, for one, resisted the temptation to throw young, bland rounds of Comté onto the market after a bare three months in the *cave,* as so many did in the postwar years. "He was mocked for aging his rounds for twelve months," Claude said. "But getting cheeses to market fast never interested him."

FROM THE MATERNELLE, Claude, Séverine, and I headed farther down into the fort. Claude began filling me in on all of the regulations Comté makers and *affineurs* follow in order to make sure Comté stays traditional: Montbéliarde cattle, copper cheesemaking kettles, spruce wood shelves in the *cave,* no artificial colorings, and so on. We passed doorways topped with dressed stone arches that led to former sleeping quarters; though they've filled the site with rack after rack of cheese, the Petite *fromagerie* has taken care to otherwise preserve the fort's original architecture. The temperature hovers between 43°F and 48°F, and must have made for a chilly night's sleep even if the *caves* are positively balmy compared to the region's sometimes bitter winter temperatures. The cheeses certainly seemed to find the conditions to their liking; the rinds we were walking among now were a deep, age-spotted mustard.

Along the corridors, stacks of Comté sat on pallets waiting to be shuffled from one *cave* to another. Claude produced a long, sharpened hollow tube of stainless steel with a wooden, T-shaped handle: a *sonde*—or "cheese iron." *Sonder* means "to sound," and the iron helps the *affineur* sound the depths of the cheese. When used with skill and knowledge, it's an invaluable tool, one that only five people at the fort get to wield. Claude began sorting through the stacked Comtés in a determined manner. He pulled a *meule* toward him, hefted it aside as if it weighed almost nothing, and did the same to the next. (When I later tried to lift a model of a Comté at a museum devoted to the cheese, I could barely budge it.) Plainly, he was looking for something. "Each cheese must be harvested at its exact moment of ripeness," he explained. Even if they're the same age, different rounds can mature differently, depending on the milk with which they were made. "There are no machines that can do this."

Claude began the judging by looking, measuring the color of the rind, and then by touching, using the surface under his flattened palm to "feel" what was happening in the middle of the cheese. "Next, you use sound," he said, hammering away with the handle end of the *sonde,* creating a noise very like that of a woodpecker thwacking the trunk of a tree.

"What sound are you listening for?" I asked.

"Here," he said, indicating the cheese he'd just tapped. The cheese "explained" the regularity of its *pâte,* he told me; the ears of *cavistes* are trained so well that they can tell by percussion alone which *fromages* to pull and which can be allowed to continue to age.

"But when it's good, when it's ready," I said, "what do you hear exactly?"

"There are little fragilities," he said. "That's what you look for."

"But," Séverine put in, grasping what I was after, "do you hear a different sound?"

Claude didn't answer. He kept tapping, passing beneath an archway into a narrow corridor to pull more rounds from the shelves there.

I turned to Séverine. "I imagine it's difficult to describe." She nodded as we watched with bemused half-grins. Then he called us to where he stood, still tapping, letting us hear for ourselves how the sound changed from one spot to another—the pitch getting slightly sharper. He'd scratched a mark on the side of the rind with a fingernail. I asked what it meant.

"Ha-hah," he said.

"It's a secret," Séverine put in.

"Evidently," I said.

"Each mark is a scan, an *échographie,* of the *fromage,*" he explained. All Comtés are "controlled." That is to say, they're judged by the *affineurs* on a scale of one to twenty as they come out of the *cave,* and a jury of professionals meets regularly to test samples from various *caves* to ensure the wheels are being sorted consistently. Comtés with scores above fifteen are banded with a green label, while rounds with a score between twelve and fifteen get a brown band. Any cheeses that come in at less than twelve can't be called Comté, and get sold as generic, non-AOC *gruyère* instead. The total is arrived at by individually scoring different aspects of the cheese: *goût* ("flavor") 9, *pâte* 5, *croûtage* 1.5, *forme* (or overall aspect) 1, and *ouverture* (i.e., holes) 3.5. Just like the cheese Olympics.

The ideal, of course, is somewhat subjective, and has shifted over time. In the 1950s, for instance, Parisians liked *meules* with lots of eyes: a picture of a *"superbe"* round from that era shows an interior with so many eyes that you almost want to reprimand it for staring. Today, however, Comtés aren't supposed to have much in the way of eyes at all. Eyes in cheese generally are the result of a bacterium called *Propionic shermanii,* which releases carbon dioxide in the *pâte.* The cheeses look different depending on conditions in the *cave*: the lower the temperature, the fewer and smaller the eyes. A good *affineur* knows how to manipulate the aging process to get a cheese that not only tastes good, but also looks the way consumers think it should.

Claude inserted the sharp end of the *sonde* into the cheese, gave it a few practiced turns, and withdrew a plug. At exactly the depth where he'd scratched a line on the outside of the rind, the slender cylinder of cheese revealed a fissure. I gave him a look of unalloyed admiration. He explained that you have to feel for the correct texture, elasticity, and firmness. "It's primordial," he said. "People are attached to the texture of things they eat." He rolled a tiny sample from the plug between his fingers, offering it to us so we could smell the yeasty, salty odor. Before replacing the plug (taking care to smear a bit of *pâte* across the wound so that it would heal), he shared bits of the sample, saying it was customary for everyone to taste.

As we chewed, Claude and Séverine refrained from speaking. "It's good" was my comment, but that didn't even begin to express what was happening in my mouth. Obviously you can't get a good cheese without good milk and an accomplished cheesemaker. But it's in the *cave,* during the aging process—the *affinage*—that a cheese's character really unfolds. The curds I tasted from Villiod's vat at the Beaufort *alpage* were nearly tasteless, after all. Aging cheese, particularly large, hard cheeses, is a bit like conjuring: One month in, and the cheese is still a blank slate. Give it a year or even two in a *cave,* under the right sort of care, however, and it can taste fabulous—and like home, at least if you come from a village in Comté. Villagers, Claude said, "recognize their own *fromage.* They may not have the vocabulary to describe why," he cautioned, yet even so, you couldn't sell the cheese from one village in another. "Every time you close a village *fromagerie,*" Claude said, "it's another *goût de fromage* that disappears from the planet."

This sort of discernment sounds fantastical, particularly given what we know about the idiosyncrasies of our palates. But while it's true our sense of taste is quite individual, there's evidence to suggest that it can be sharpened. The nose, you may recall, plays a key role in taste; most of what we experience while eating something is the result of "retronasal" information. And no matter its limitations, the nose is not a complete lost cause. In one study (which must have been as much fun to conduct as it must also have been to watch), people were asked to follow a trail of chocolate essential oil through a field, nose to ground, hunting-dog style, while blindfolded and wearing earplugs. Two-thirds of them could do it. Even better, for those who completed a series of successive doggie runs over a few days, their times nearly doubled. Our noses, and by extension our taste buds, can indeed be trained.

And at the Poligny branch of the Institut National de la Recherche Agronomique, in Franche-Comté, they're busy training them. One of the main aims of INRA-Poligny's work is to determine how different production methods affect the flavor of cheeses. In a mini-*fromagerie* equipped with miniature silver vats and miniature curd-cutters, test batches are fed to researchers sitting in walled-off cubicles. Samples are passed through a little sliding door into an interior lit with a red light so that the cheese's color doesn't affect taste impressions. Trainees then mark those impressions ("bitter, acid, salty, sugary, metallic" and so on) on a "Sensory Training Analysis" sheet. Poligny takes taste so seriously that it even has a machine that can make a "smell-o-graph" of a cheese's aromas. (The research facility is also where Mother Noëlla Marcellino, an American Benedictine nun and cheese microbiologist—aka "The Cheese Nun"—spent several years researching what turned out to be a wide diversity of strains of bacteria in various *caves* in the Massif Central, all of which can also contribute to the unique flavor of a particular cheese.)

The result is that no other region devotes more time to taste training, or discusses it in more detail, than Franche-Comté. Next door to the INRA labs, at a small museum called the Maison du Comté, guides attempt to educate visitors in the art of tasting by having them smell various scents. (I identified hay and nutmeg and honey before my olfactory abilities failed me.) And one booklet on Comté tasting that I picked up while in the region contains no fewer than seven pages discussing taste. On one was a "Wheel of Aromas," with six taste families broken down into eighty-three descriptors. "Lactic," for instance, included "fresh milk, cooked milk, acidified curd, rancid butter, fresh cream" and so on; "vegetable" had "hay, wet hay, straw, garlic, fermented grass, artichoke, endive and soil"; "animal" included "meat stock, stable at milking time, and wet wool"; and "roasted" broke down into things as varied as "fresh bread crust, brioche bread, fried onion, burnt onion, coffee, coffee with milk, fudge, toasted bread, tobacco, chicory, roasted peanut," and so on. The booklet cautioned that although the lists were extensive, they weren't meant to be exhaustive.

As I stood chewing the sample of Comté Claude had given me, it was clear I would have to devote considerably more time to smelling various aromas before I reached such prowess. To my far less experienced tongue, the Comté had an edge of Swiss-y-ness, combined with the familiar *gruyère* notes of roasted nuts and caramelized onions, as if an American-style Swiss and a Beaufort had had babies. But of course, they hadn't. What had happened was that a round of almost flavorless solidified milk had come into the *caves*. Then Claude, and Claude's team of *affineurs* (and their robots) had brushed it and turned it and moved it from *cave* to *cave,* making sure it was at just the right temperature and humidity, so that the bacteria inside the cheese could work their way through the *pâte,* transforming it until what had once been bland curd became something else entirely. They had done this not to a hundred, nor to thousands, but to tens of thousands of rounds of cheese. And that is what you might call magic.

BASTARD CAVES AND
ROTTEN BREAD

~~~~~~~~~~~~~

"Cheese, like oil, makes too much of itself."

—JEROME K. JEROME

O n a topographical map, the whole of France's mountainous middle, the Massif Central, resembles a prehistoric
spearhead, its flinty tip balanced precariously on the Mediter-
ranean coast. Near this arrow's southernmost end spreads the
unyielding limestone plateau known as the Grand Causse du
Larzac—the largest, most arid, and least hospitable of all the
causses. The royal charter that granted Roquefort cheese its ear-
liest name protection described this area as *ce terroir où ne pousse
ni pied de vigne, ni grain de blé*—"the place where neither vines nor
grains of wheat grow." Wind-battered, rock-fractured, and red-

dish, the earth here is stippled with stalks of teasel, whose genus name, *Dipsacus,* comes from the word for thirst.

Among these scoured, parched lands, in a crease of earth that nuzzles one edge of the Combalou mountain, lies the village of Roquefort-sur-Soulzon. Slim ribbons of road wind through the canted plains to the village, and on my way into the region, I had passed what looked like old tires buried partway into a slight rise. They'd been painted white and arranged to form the message *"OGM, Non, non et non"*—"Genetically Modified Organisms, No, no and no." If *terroir* breeds a sort of person, the Roquefort *terroir* has shaped a particularly truculent type. It's unsurprising, therefore, that the area was at the center of one of the most famous uprisings against American food imperialism ever to occur on French soil. Or that its cheese has attracted defenders such as José Bové, sometime sheep farmer and (as he was once dubbed by *Outside* magazine) "badass environmentalist."

Bové was the architect of the dismantling of a McDonald's under construction in Millau, the largest town near the Roquefort *caves*. Wearing a T-shirt emblazoned with the crimson sheep logo of the Roquefort sheep farmers' association, he set out with a group of fellow agriculturalists one August morning in 1999, riding tractors and forklifts to the site of the almost finished restaurant, where with "chainsaws, chisels and screwdrivers, the crowd, kids too, set about removing windows, prying off tiles, dismantling walls and taking down signs," wrote Florence Williams in *Outside.* The scene was a food purist's dream, and the whole thing, she observed, was made for television: "There was Bové, lugging around a broken McDonald's sign bigger than he was. There was the parade of farm vehicles loaded with debris, which was gently deposited on the lawn of the Millau regional prefecture. There were the farmwives, cheerfully passing out Roquefort snacks to drivers and passersby."

The choice of *fromage* didn't merely reflect what locals had on hand for a tasty protest *hors d'œuvre*. The thing that had really whipped up tempers—for which McDonald's was simply a convenient stand-in—was a punitive U.S. import tax of 100 percent on Roquefort (along with a long list of other suspiciously effete French foods such as mustard, foie gras, and shallots), imposed in response to France's refusal to accept hormone-laced American beef. Bové justified the retaliation by saying, "McDonald's is the symbol of the standardization of food." What he failed to mention is that no other traditional *fromage* offers such a challenge to traditionalists' claims that the most authentic cheeses are the ones that have remained the least touched by science, technology, and big business. Because if there's a symbol of the standardization of traditional French cheese, it's Roquefort.

A SINGLE SPORE of *Penicillium roqueforti* may be invisible to the naked eye; even so, the microscopic beasties are wholly responsible for the clutter of buildings lining the narrow streets of Roquefort-sur-Soulzon; the entire skinny village springs from mold. Above the office buildings and restaurants and houses, the Combalou—from the Gaulish *combal,* for "saddle"—stretches for over a mile and a half, and all Roquefort in the world comes from this one craggy escarpment of rock. Some two hundred million years ago, part of the mountain collapsed, leaving a massive jumble of cliff and stone, underneath which lie the Roquefort *caves.* Some of these extend eleven stories into the earth, forming a second, unseen village beneath the village devoted to cheese.

In the middle of town sits an unassuming, squarish box of brick—the entrance to the *caves* owned by Société, the largest maker of Roquefort. An elevator took me several stories down to a large subterranean room, where a tour kicked off with the French idea of proper educational display: a *spectacle son et lumière.* First, a topographical model large enough to fill one side of the room lit up. The model looked as though it had been constructed from blocks made of papier-mâché or foam, like those miniature volcanoes from grade school that were supposed to teach you about geology, but that only demonstrated how cool it was to make fake lava flows with Alka-Seltzer. As a busload of spectators and I stood watching, half of the model began to move. The blocks rumbled impressively before settling to reveal what could only be the sheer, crimp-faced hump of the Combalou. The lights went down, and a white strobe flashed to signal the passing millennia. A long, sustained note—akin to a synthesized church choir singing "Ahhhh"—shimmered, then modulated into pulsating crescendos like the soundtrack from a 1950s sci-fi film when the main character is caught in a space vortex that will either save him or transform him into something monstrous. Then: dawn. Birds calling, crickets chirping, the crowing of a rooster. The lights went back up to reveal, as if through the providence of some great foam-model deity, the village of Roquefort perched on the flanks of the Combalou. The group cried, "Ah!"

A little farther along on the tour, the story of how Roquefort came to be made in those flanks was told through a second sound-and-light show. As some very dramatic stringed instruments played in the background, a shepherd, represented by a distorted tan image projected onto a rock wall, appeared, while a shepherdess-shaped white light fled up a nearby stairwell. As the legend had it, the young herder was so overcome by the lass's beauty that he stashed the rucksack holding his lunch of curd and bread in a cleft of the Combalou mountain in order to pursue her. When he came back some months later to retrieve his satchel, he found that his curd had been transformed into the wonder that would become known as Roquefort, the world's most famous *bleu*.

This amorous scene was followed by the strikes of a hammer over a fervent choral score, accompaniment for more sound-and-light-show imagery that told how the mountain's natural grottos had been converted into proper aging rooms. The group and I stood, stories below sunken stories, in one of those constructed rooms, which featured an impressive series of vaults and stone columns stage-lit in honeyed hues—yet another almost hallowed-feeling space devoted to French cheese.

Société owns 90 percent of all the *caves* in the Combalou, including a series of inimitable, high-vaulted chambers, capable of holding twenty-seven thousand rounds. The *caves* feature heavily in the company's promotional materials, and I came upon one such poster while walking up and down Roquefort's slanted streets. It depicted round after creamy round lying in snug rows under an arched stone ceiling, presided over by Société advertising icon Maurice Astruc. A beefy-cheeked, mustachioed man in a beret and blue peasant smock, Astruc cuts a figure of such stunning rusticity that even the French have to be assured that he's real and did indeed work for Société as a *maître affineur* for some forty years.

If Roquefort itself is so well known that its very name is essentially synonymous with blue cheese—having long nearly eclipsed all other French blues, and only recently given ground to English Stilton and Italian Gorgonzola—the pretty *caves* and Maurice with his mustache have helped to make the name Société synonymous with "Roquefort." Originally known as the Société Civile des Caves Réunies (later renamed Société des Caves et des Producteurs Réunis de Roquefort), the "society" was created by a group of *affineurs* in 1842 at the beginning of a general consolidation in Roquefort making. Société's green-and-white oval logo adorns the cheese aisle of practically every *supermarché* in France, and if you've actually found Roquefort at your local grocery store in the United States, it was likely packaged in one of Société's distinctive green plastic wedges.

The brand is so ubiquitous that the *Larousse des Fromages* laments that "many French aren't aware that there isn't just one Roquefort." And if Société had its way, it's possible there wouldn't be. In the 1930s there were still eight hundred dairies churning out rounds of Roquefort to be aged. Today there are just eight. Papillon—the other brand offering tours of *caves* used for actual Roquefort aging—has 11 percent of total Roquefort production, while the five smaller brands split less than 20 percent of the market. The remaining 70-some percent of all Roquefort comes from the two dairies owned by Société.

Of that Roquefort, 80 to 90 percent is what Société calls "Roquefort Depuis 1863" (after the year they patented the green-and-white oval logo). In a small *dégustation* at the *caves,* we began with the 1863 and progressed to the "Roquefort Caves des Templiers" and "Roquefort Cave des Baragnaudes." As I placed a morsel of 1863 on my tongue, I had the impression of one very strong *bleu.* The second cheese, the Templiers, was even stronger (definitely living up to its ad copy "strong like the Templars") and was riddled with a strain of mold so darkly green as to be nearly black. Finally came the Baragnaudes, the strongest—so sharp it induced near shivers. To the man next to me in the tasting line, I said, "They're getting stronger."

"Yes," he agreed. "*On monte,*" though the Baragnaudes—the

name comes from the Occitan for "fairy"—is in fact supposed to be the mildest, with only a smattering of clear, bottle-green mold.

In any case, each called to mind words such as *brawny, assertive,* maybe even *virile.* In a tasting, Roquefort is always the ending point—it will crush any other cheese and probably your wine, too. It's so strong that people have been known to add butter to their Roquefort in an attempt to dampen the flavor. Patrick Rance wrote of this "deplorable but common custom" with some derision: "I am used to eating butter under cheese (like the Normans), but mixing it, never. It spoils both." (When I later mentioned buttering the cheese to a native of the area, he said, "Those people weren't from Roquefort.")

The remnants of 2,700-year-old molds for shaping cheese have been found in the Roquefort area, and given the harshness of the Larzac, it's not difficult to imagine ancient people being willing to eat those cheeses even if they had sprouted a little fuzz. Extreme hunger has certainly been offered up as a possible explanation for why anyone would consider eating a food shot through with freakish blue-green spores. I've heard there are some who won't go near blue cheese for that very reason, though I myself have a hard time comprehending such squeamishness. Alongside all those factory-produced, rectangular blocks of cheddar in my Wisconsin cheese youth, there was also a lot of *bleu*—great moist globs of it topping absolutely every salad my mother ever ordered at a restaurant. I can still picture her forking up mouthfuls, those moldy, ambrosial crumbs balanced on the tines.

Each variety of Roquefort produced by Société is aged in a separate *cave,* and the differences between *caves* do play a subtle role in the taste. In spite of constant efforts by *affineurs* to fine-tune the atmosphere, conditions in each *cave* can vary—even with all the remodeling, the inside of the Combalou is still the inside of a mountain. You could see this in the large cavern where the tour group and I had watched the shepherd and shepherdess story. At one end beckoned the entrance to a *fleurine*: long, jagged openings that formed with the crumbling of the Combalou's north face. Surface air enters through these shafts, where it is both cooled and moistened through contact with a subterranean aquifer; the entire formation is essentially a giant natural swamp cooler. The air flow helps maintain the *caves* at a chilly 48°F or so and more than 95 percent humidity. Ideal conditions, that is, for aging Roquefort.

The conditions were less ideal for tourists, and as we walked through a dank passageway, past rocks sprigged with moss and ferns, people blew their noses and sniffled. We shuffled into a stoop-ceilinged *cave* full of oaken racks. The guide, a chipper brunette with a lilting voice, held aloft a bottle reminiscent of those in which the minutiae-minded construct sailing vessels. This bottle, however, contained a hunk of bluish bread: the culturing grounds for Société's *Penicillium roqueforti,* the real determining factor in how a Roquefort tastes. Each producer cultivates his own secret strains, and each strain makes for a slightly different Roquefort. Société harvests its mold from these bottles, but down the road, rival cheesemaker Papillon actually still sets bread to mold in the *caves* themselves. Each year, a baker crisps several hundred loaves in a very hot oven, turning the crusts sooty while leaving the insides yeasty. These loaves are then seeded with Papillon's mold strain and left in the *caves* for forty days, after which the *Penicillium roqueforti* is extracted from the moldy innards. (The strains are quality-tested in a lab before hitting the cheese.) During my visit to Papillon, the guide showed us half a dozen large, blackened rounds of rye bread, each looking rather like the severed top of some unspeakable fungus.

Once harvested, the spores are added to the milk at the dairy. After the curd has been cut, inseminated, and molded, it's considered a *pain*—or "loaf." These are bigger than you might think if you've only ever seen wedges of Roquefort—a full round weighs a hefty five or six pounds and has the circumference of your typical fruitcake tin. Each, of course, is a sort of Roquefort blank: a Roquefort waiting to happen. The *pains* are drained and salted, and then they're ready for the *piquage*.

The process of *piquage* was invented by one Antoine Roussel, of the village of Laqueuille, a man apparently more observant and determined than most. While studying his cheese sometime around 1850, he noted that the blue was more pronounced in the cracks and crevices. Motivated by these observations, writes French biologist and cheese historian Jean Froc, he "applied himself during long months to looking for a way to systemati-cally blue the *pâte*." Eventually, Roussel hit upon the ingenious, if vaguely diabolical, idea of piercing the cheeses to allow air and *Penicillium* to better penetrate the interior of the cheese. This new and improved *bleuing* was considered no small matter: In the village of Laqueuille (where he also served as mayor for three decades), framed by two plane trees in a little square next to the church, stands a bust of Roussel complete with a plaque describ-ing his achievement.

Though Roussel conducted his experiments in Auvergne, using a cheese known as Bleu de Laqueuille, it wasn't long before Roquefort makers started sticking their cheeses with needles as well, soon aided further by the *machine à piquer,* a disk bristling with forty-some long, blunt metal needles that is lowered onto a cheese, impaling the *pâte.* Cut open any mature *bleu* that has un-dergone *piquage,* and you'll see the faint tracks from the needles in the long slashes of mold.

After they've been needled, the *pains* go to the *caves.* In the old days, men delivering *pains* from the dairies would lob the unwrapped rounds through the air from the top of a truck's bed to a partner on the ground, as if they were misshapen soccer balls. Once inside the *caves,* the rounds are placed on their sides on oaken racks. The wood absorbs moisture and helps maintain an even humidity. (Apparently just getting the shelving material can be a tricky matter, at least if one maker whom Rance spoke with is to be believed. According to him, "The oak must be cut at full moon in a North wind, and only from October to March, when no sap is rising.") Once set on these very particular shelves, Roquefort is aged a minimum of three months, including the two weeks they spend *à poil*—"naked" on the shelves—preening their pale, bluey selves. After the master *affineurs* judge them ready, the rounds are *plombés*—"tinned." To demonstrate, our guide took a round of polished wood and wrapped it smartly in a square piece of tinfoil—aluminum is too light—first folding the four corners over the cheese, then the four puffy sides of the paper before rolling the block on its side to tamp it all down. A seasoned wrapper can wrap 100 Roqueforts per hour, or about 750 a day.

The aged, wrapped rounds go into refrigeration, which greatly decelerates the rate at which the *Penicillium* spores consume the *pâte*. Roquefort *affinage* takes place roughly from January to July, when the sheep are providing milk. By the fall, all the rounds have been moved to cold storage, and the *caves* lie empty (although some of the racks at Société sported the odd fake round or three for the benefit of the tourists). Patrick Rance felt this *momification* "denatured" the *fromage,* but the *plombé* method—which dates to the spread of refrigeration in the early twentieth century—has become standard.

As the Société tour wound down, we passed through the "museum," a section of tunnel featuring mannequins and copper milk jugs, an old milking machine, a *machine à piquer,* and the little carts that were once used to trundle *pains* about the *caves*. At the very end, set in openings in the rock, was a series of life-size dioramas of famous personages with a Roquefort connection. There was Pliny, whose mention of "the most esteemed *fromage* in Rome" in 76 CE is thought to refer to Roquefort; Charlemagne, who had, you'll recall, helped make the cheese famous; and Diderot, who praised Roquefort in his encyclopedia. The very last vignette was Casanova, arrayed in a purple coat with lace cuffs, offering half a Roquefort to a woman. We had come full circle from Roquefort's passionate beginnings, and returned to the subject of *amour.* "Casanova," the guide explained as we gazed at the tableau, "was convinced that if you had Roquefort, all that remained was to pick out *la dame.*" The crowd guffawed before heading upstairs and out.

AFTER LEAVING THE CAVES, I detoured through nearby Millau. Near the gateway to the town was a traffic circle adorned with a sign: a cheery flaxen *M* on a Ronald-red background. "Is that the McDonald's?" I asked Robert Glandières the following day. Yes, he said, that was it, "the famous one."

Robert, along with his wife, Martine, is a Roquefort sheep farmer. They own, in common with several other families, some 520 sheep. They also have a couple of bed-and-breakfast rooms. One afternoon during my stay with them, Robert and I settled onto a set of velour sofa and chairs in his living room, not far from the table where I'd taken to filching the Glandièreses' nearly grown children's Nutella rather than eating the *confiture maison* Martine laid out so nicely near my place setting each morning. Robert—who has spiky brown hair and was wearing green denim pants and a green cable-knit sweater that made him look like a rangy stalk of asparagus—just happened to be the current president of the Fédération Régionale des Syndicats des Eleveurs de Brebis. He was, that is, the head honcho for all the sheep farmers who produce milk for Roquefort.

The sheep, like the cheese, are historic. They're called Lacaunes, and you can see them on postcards in every souvenir shop throughout Aveyron (the main *département* in the authorized zone for Roquefort milk collection). Usually they're shown clustered picturesquely around a *lavagne,* a small pond for watering livestock that people used to make by deliberately cobbling natural depressions in a landscape with little moisture to spare. Sheep generally produce less milk than goats, and far, far less milk than cows. But though the quantity is less, sheep's milk, with its high fat and protein content, is far richer. Combine this with the relatively short lactation cycle of sheep, and you begin to understand why sheep's milk—and in particular, milk for Roquefort—is so expensive.

But Lacaunes are milk-giving super-sheep, at least compared to the several historical breeds from the Larzac out of which they were bred in the 1920s. In 1875 a good milking sheep produced 33 liters of milk per season, while the average was 14. Today a single Lacaune averages 220 liters of milk per season.

That level of production is both good and bad, according to Glandières. Roquefort producers don't actually make as much Roquefort as they could. Instead, in recent years companies have augmented their lines with other sheep's-milk products. Modern French people, Glandières explained, sometimes skip the cheese course altogether. He also noted that Roquefort is a less-than-convenient cocktail snack: sticky blue crumbles make for a tough finger food.

As a consequence, Roquefort producers still hold out hope for a bigger market share on our side of the pond. Hence the outrage over the U.S. luxury tax. And as if the first tax—which came out of the Clinton administration—weren't enough, one of the last acts of the George W. Bush administration was to propose a new, 300 percent luxury tax on the cheese. If it had gone through, some Roqueforts—such as L'Aigle Noir, produced by Carles (the connoisseur's maker, boasting the most "by-hand" production of all the brands), would have retailed for more than $100 per pound in the States, assuming it could be obtained at all. Roquefort producers and their supporters were outraged. "We're being picked on," one told the BBC. Even José Bové got back into the action, leading a delegation that delivered Roquefort to the U.S. embassy in Paris. For good measure, a box of Roquefort was also sent to the White House to show President Obama firsthand just what the American public would be missing.

The U.S. market is so important, Glandières said, that after the original tax went through, the Roquefort sheep farmers voluntarily took a reduced price on the portion of their milk destined for the United States, hoping this sacrifice would help the cheese to retain a toehold. U.S. officials ultimately agreed to axe the proposed new tax—though only in exchange for a quadrupling of imports of American beef to France. Such tactics do make it easier to understand why sheep farmers would line up to assist Bové (who was at the time a member of the federation) with the dismantling of the McDonald's, even if as a whole they really aren't into "*des actions commando*," as Glandières put it. Besides, it was a "Mac Doh" we were talking about. Glandières gave me a wry look across the coffee table. "They're intelligent," he said of the fast-food chain, "and they know how to adapt."

I knew what he meant. I rarely eat at a McDonald's in the States, and when I do, it always seems to be almost by accident, as if a fried-food black hole opened and suddenly, unaware, I'm eating a Filet-O-Fish. And yet I found myself seeking out the golden arches across France. I suspect my reasons for doing so were similar to French reasons. The Mac Dohs were located in well-marked spots right off the highway. They served food no matter what time of day I happened to be looking for lunch, even if it was at ten minutes until twelve. A meal there cost about a quarter what it did anywhere else, and I wasn't expected to linger over it for two hours. Then there was the real clincher: free public WiFi—still a rarity in the French countryside. Beyond these draws, the "look" of a French McDonald's is, well, hip. In fact, you have to wonder if the one sure result of the bad feeling stirred in French consumers by incidents such as the Roquefort farmers' assault wasn't to spur improvements to the chain's décor. As part of an effort to increase the appeal of McDonald's restaurants to Europeans, the company created a studio near Paris that cranks out stylish design concepts with names such as "Eternity" and "Pure and Simple."

Certainly the farmers' demonstration doesn't seem to have had much effect otherwise. McDonald's continues to be undeniably popular in France. The country is the franchise's number two market after the United States, with more than 1,100 locations, including 70 in Paris alone. In 2008, in the midst of the economic crisis, McDonald's revenue in France rose 11 percent. The phenomenon is observable: Every single McDonald's I walked into in France—and I mean every one, everywhere— was absolutely packed with French diners at mealtimes. I'd never seen anything like it anywhere in the States.

And the image of Roquefort farmers as rebellious peasants against this sort of industrial food takeover is not exactly accurate. There is no such thing as farmhouse Roquefort. All of it is industrially made. Starting in the mid- to late 1880s, and led by the producers who had grouped together to create Société, Roquefort makers did everything they could to ensure greater and greater market shares for their cheese. Nor were their methods necessarily in keeping with what we've come to think of as sustainable, tradition-conscious practices. For example, as demand for Roquefort grew, the collection zone for

Roquefort milk was extended far beyond the cheese's original *terroir,* first to Corsica in 1893 and then to the Pyrenees in 1910. The expanded collection zone remained in place, despite complaints in both areas that the diversion of milk for Roquefort hurt local peasants—there was less milk for local cheesemakers, which meant fewer rounds and higher prices at village markets. Roquefort farmers and makers were also among the first to implement automatic milking machines; by the 1930s, rudimentary setups had appeared in barns across the region. And they were keen to take advantage of other technological advances, wiring the *caves* for electricity and installing refrigeration units as soon as they were able. This, combined with the use of the tinfoil wrappers, allowed makers to stock greater quantities of cheese, which meant Roquefort ceased to be a seasonal delicacy and became available year-round.

In the *caves* themselves, women known as *cabanières* composed 90 percent of the workforce. Though often presented as a picturesque part of the history of the cheese, photos of *cabanières* show bevies of grim-faced ladies wearing stiff full-length aprons over their clothing and wooden shoes to protect their feet from the constant belowground chill. Most came from area farms and were engaged for the season in advance, often taking room and board in strictly run dormitories presided over by nuns. One day per week they got to see the sky; the rest of the time they lived like moles underground: schlepping cheeses from room to room, scraping rinds, wrapping, packing.

By the early twentieth century, one observer complained that Roquefort had become *"une énorme machine industrielle et commerciale,"* which every day got further and further from agriculture. Nor did this machine tolerate imitators. So when some enterprising individuals began making faux versions of the cheese (as you may recall, such difficulties had plagued Roquefort since the late Middle Ages), aging them in what were called *caves bâtardes*—"bastard caves"—Roquefort makers mobilized to seal Roquefort's name protection once and for all by securing that first, very early, official AOC for cheese in 1925. For good measure, not long afterward they also obtained a decree recognizing the Roquefort AOC from the U.S. government.

Recent decades have seen a movement among cheese professionals across France to turn AOCs into true mechanisms for preserving history, tradition, and the environment—for example, by adding provisions that would require herders to return to natural grazing pastures. In the case of Roquefort, rules have been revised to decrease the size of the milk collection zone and to respect the natural lactation cycle of the Lacaunes. But if name protection in and of itself kept a cheese pure and simple, as many traditionalists suggest, then people would still be making Roquefort in little shacks near a handy fissure of the Combalou, in a peasant paradise of bucolic splendor.

This is not, of course, what happened. AOC in hand, Roquefort industrialists began buying up makers not only of fake Roquefort, but of other blue cheeses in the region, such as Bleu des Causses. The acquisition mania culminated in 1992, when Société itself was gobbled up by none other than Lactalis. Over time, the farmers, too, organized themselves into the sheep farmers' federation, and business practices around Roquefort became strict, even monopolistic. Today all the farms milking for Roquefort belong to the federation and all the dairies belong to an analogous group. The farms sell only to the dairies, and the dairies buy only from the farms. Each year, the two meet to determine the price of milk for the next year; during my stay, Glandières was knee-deep in negotiations. And while it's hard to know what José Bové's exact motives may have been—he's often accused of an overfondness for media attention—even he stopped milking for Roquefort on the grounds that the cheese was too industrial. After the McDonald's incident, Glandières said, Bové "left the Fédération *de suite.*"

Nor have Roquefort makers eschewed science. Like *gruyère* and Camembert, as a "chosen" cheese of France, Roquefort benefitted from the concentrated efforts of technicians. Makers used the resulting advances into mold research to fine-tune their product, ensuring that the cheese itself became more and more standardized. And in 1948, as the FDA was on the brink of outlawing all raw milk cheeses in the United States, it was the Roquefort industrials who called in scientific experts to testify that two months' aging could ensure the safety of raw-milk cheeses. (Roquefort, recall, is aged at least three months.) Hence the United States' sixty-day rule.

It would be an overstatement to say that all of this makes Roquefort exactly like McDonald's, but there are certain parallels to be drawn. It's even difficult to argue that Roquefort is the healthier option. One hundred grams of a Big Mac contains 273 calories. And one hundred grams of Roquefort contains 369 calories. Admittedly, most people are unlikely to eat a hundred grams of blue cheese (nearly a quarter of a pound) at one sitting, while a hundred grams of a Big Mac is less than half a burger. And the cheese does beat out the Big Mac in terms of protein, vitamin A, and calcium, plus it has fewer carbohydrates to boot. Even so, it's considerably higher in fat, sodium, and cholesterol. Roquefort may not be *la malbouffe*—"junk food"—but it's not exactly celery sticks, either.

All in all, as I traveled around listening to yet another French person grumble that they send us Americans beautiful food while in return we give them *conneries,* I got rather weary of the French heaping of an American-style world-food takeover solely at our feet. Standardization and the desire to protect and expand one's brand are not exclusively American tendencies. No other cheese has ever known the level of name protection that Roquefort has known. It's the culmination of an AOC, the culmination of a French tradition. And it's fully industrialized.

BEFORE I LEFT the Glandières farm, Martine took me to see the sheep barn. She showed me the milking machine, a circular, rotating platform capable of milking hundreds of sheep per hour. On a nearby wall hung the milk collection register; during high-fabrication season, the milk truck rumbles in once a day to transport the milk to one of the dairies that supplies Société with rounds for aging. We walked to a pen filled with young sheep, who sniffed and snuffed my hands, then started nibbling to see if I might be something good to eat. Martine said some of their guests occasionally asked to see the animals, though many more came for the *Saut à l'élastique*. One of the real draws in Roquefort land these days, in other words, is not its *patrimoine gastronomique*, but its bungee jumping.

Patrick Rance once called the *fleurines* that riddle the Combalou "great sinister cracks." The entire mountain, in a sense, is flawed, but it's the flaws in the mountain that make the cheese possible. If, as humans, we're to have any hope of preserving our heritage, we can do so only by looking at what it is and what it isn't, head on—even as powerful industrial syndicates and standardization complicate the idea of traditional *fromage*. Leaving Martine to her chores, I walked along the lane leading away from the barn, pausing to contemplate the rocky crags that bordered early autumn pastures bleached so pale they were nearly the color of bone. Though I couldn't see them, I knew that somewhere out there the *lavagnes*—those placid, spheroid pools that dot the Larzac—confronted the unsparing sun with gazes of unblinking blue.

THE OLD SHEEPHERDER

~~~~~~~~~

"Blessed are the cheesemakers."

—MONTY PYTHON, *LIFE OF BRIAN*

It is worth remembering that the bells worn by dairy animals—cowbells and goat bells and sheep bells—aren't just meant to be pretty. They're meant to help herders locate wandering animals, a sort of aural reconnoitering, a way in which what's lost might be found. And in the Pyrenees, that distant scrim of mountains on the horizon line between France and Spain, shepherds are said to have near-superhuman bell-identification powers. "For many a *berger*," writes Patrick Rance, "the bell identifies at a distance the size and sex of a straying beast [. . .] some shepherds can detect the absence of a single sheep bell from among a flock of a thousand." I never thought to ask René

Miramon if he had this ability, though I wouldn't be surprised to learn he did. Instead, we talked about a different superpower of his, namely: in a land in which even one of the oldest cheeses on record is thoroughly industrial, and where hand-milking is so scarce that it has to be staged for the cameras, René Miramon still makes his cheeses and milks his sheep by hand.

AS YOU APPROACH the Pyrenees, the French landscape starts to feel attenuated, as if someone has taken the Hexagon and stretched it until only serrated peaks and scraps of cloud remain. Being there felt like being at the edge of the world, as if it might be possible to tumble over the ridgeline of the mountains into nothingness. In reality, of course, I would only have tumbled into Spain, which is less than ten miles from the village of Bedous. Bedous is at the head of one of many long creases of land that lie perpendicular to the spine of the Pyrenees, forming *le peigne*—"the comb"—that separates the foothills into strandlike valleys. I happened to be there in the spring, when the gray- and white- and bone-colored buildings of the village stood out against tufts of brilliantly green grass and the still-empty rakes of espaliered trees looked expectant above rows of glossy hedges. According to the French government, the hamlet lies in the Aspe Valley, in the Pyrénées-Atlantiques *département*; locals, however, are more apt to say they live in the old region of Béarn. According to one Basque priest who spoke to Rance, people have been making *brebis*—"sheep's-milk cheese"—in the mountains along the border for some four thousand years. That claim may be specious, but no matter. No one doubts that cheese has been made in the Pyrenees for a really long time.

Along the middle of the valley runs a *route nationale,* and everything in Bedous is either "near the *nationale*" or "just off the *nationale*." I didn't bother calling ahead for directions; once I arrived in Bedous, I simply stopped at the local *boulangerie* and asked the baker how to get to my bed-and-breakfast. It was around the corner, off the *nationale,* and turned out to be a cavernous place of gray stucco with a tower and lots of dark wood paneling. Jean-Claude Teisseire, and his wife, who was related to the once-prominent family who'd built the overlarge structure, had converted part of the home into a guesthouse, installing shower stalls and sinks into odd corners of the bedrooms. When Jean-Claude, a tall, whiskery man with black eyebrows, asked after my plans, and I explained that I'd come to Bedous looking for *brebis,* he said, "Ah!" and jabbed a long finger ceilingward. "I'll just go call the shepherd."

THE FOLLOWING MORNING, Jean-Claude rode along in my car to show me the way down the *nationale* to the farm of the Miramons: cheesemakers and his friends. Their green-roofed barn and *fromagerie* sat in a field at the edge of the village. At the door to the milk room, we were met by Régine Miramon, tomboyish and wiry in a striped sweater, blue jeans, and a stunning pair of true-white go-go-girl-style rubber cheesemaking boots. As we stepped inside, her husband, Jean-Louis—René's son—appeared. When he saw me, he said, *"Je suis le berger"*—"I am the shepherd." Then he shook my hand very politely, as though I were a visiting dignitary. He was outfitted in the coveralls French farmers don when mucking about with their dairy animals, and a pair of gold-rimmed aviator sunglasses. (So that his wife would later tease, "Hey, a peasant in sunglasses?") The collar of the dark shirt he wore beneath the coverall was flipped up, and a five o'clock shadow darkened his jaw. He looked like Tom Cruise in *Top Gun*.

Youthful and energetic, the Miramons are part of a small but determined group of younger people moving back to the land. They'd both had office jobs, but decided to return to Bedous to take up sheep farming. I'd met others like them across the country: a freckle-faced Melissa Gilbert look-alike in Provence who had bought a herd of goats in order to make Banon, the *chèvre* that comes wrapped in chestnut leaves; a woman in Burgundy who'd begun making *fermier* Époisses; a trio of brothers in Auvergne making farmhouse Bleu d'Auvergne.

The Miramon farm, originally owned by Jean-Louis's grandparents, dates to a time when townspeople would trundle out in the evenings with their bottles and other containers to collect a share of the milk supplied by the dairy cows. It was their son René who turned the operation toward sheep and *fromage de brebis.* The younger generation continues the family cheese-making, though things have changed some. The day I visited it, the milk parlor was chock full of professional-grade stainless-steel equipment, including large vats outfitted with temperature gauges and digital readouts. When I followed Régine into her cheesemaking room, I found a huge stainless-steel kettle that stood as high as her waist. It was equipped with a mechanized arm to which she could attach mixing paddles and other tools, as if it were a giant KitchenAid mixer.

I'd arrived just after the milking, and I watched as Régine added her rennet, then hit a button to set the arm on the machine spinning; the milk needed to be well blended so that the fat would not separate out. After a few moments, she stopped the equipment. "We need to leave it for twenty-five minutes or so," she told me, noting the time. "We can go see the animals while we wait." In the barn, close to two hundred sheep stood in a long pen, heads stuck down and away in their feeding troughs, so that the only thing visible was a long line of fluffy sun-striped *brebis* rear ends. As is the case with *chèvre,* the word *brebis* refers to both the cheese and the female animal that produces the milk. The ones the Miramons own are Basco-Béarnaise, the *race locale.* They had long, mournful white faces, with black eyes set high in their heads and horns curling over each ear. Occasionally they gazed upward as if they knew too much and pitied us humans in a placid, ovine way.

The Aspe is the middle valley of five that make up the AOC

zone for Ossau-Iraty, the protected name for a *tomme de brebis* from the Pyrenees. The appellation, which dates to 1980, lumps together the Ossau Valley—one valley to the east of the Aspe—and the Iraty Forest, located in Basque country. Rance, ever the purist, considered combining even the cheeses from Ossau with those of Iraty (let alone those from all five valleys) to be a travesty: "To group them together because both are made of ewes' milk in the modern *département* of Pyrénées-Atlantiques is rather like lumping Chopin together with Tchaikovsky because both lived under Russian rule and both were composers." When I asked Régine what she called her cheese, however, she shrugged and said it was *tomme de pays*—"country cheese." Like lots of producers who sell only locally, she and Jean-Louis hadn't gotten an AOC certification, though she said with a decidedly speculative air that the AOC was "something to think about."

At the end of the barn the doors stood open to the warming weather; in the early summer months, the sheep go outside to graze. But, Régine explained, "There's not much land here in the valley, you see." So in July, René still makes the *transhumance* to the high pastures, the *estives,* still walks alongside his sheep into the hills. In recent decades it's become popular in France to hold *transhumance* festivals, even if the *transhumance* isn't quite what it once was, or never happened at all, as was the case in the town I visited in the Jura. I went to another such festival that featured a *bal des bergers*—a "shepherds' ball"—with music provided by a DJ outfit calling itself Power Night Animation, a ski lift offering panoramic views of livestock, and a contingent of clowns. There were also some two thousand sheep. They walked clumped together as though their coats were made of Velcro, a carpet of cream-colored bouclé unfurling past fields of red poppies, heading up a road toward the ski resort above. Though it was undeniably cool to see them (if not so cool to walk in their poo-spattered wake), they'd been staged at the head of the route, brought up in trucks that could just as easily have driven them the rest of the way.

In the Alps, meanwhile, at the much-touted Retour des Alpages held by the city of Annecy, the relatively short *transhumance* mostly seems to be an opportunity to eat *tartiflette géante* and drink lots of beer. In fact, there's only one other place I know of in France besides the Pyrenees where they still make an authentically arduous trek into the mountains, and that's Corsica. The *transhumance* there is the work of one stubborn guy who has decided to persist. They made a film of him.

Régine and I walked back toward the cheesemaking room. On a stainless-steel table sat the eleven cheeses she'd molded the previous day, a typical number for the spring. Each round weighed about ten pounds and was about four inches high; they were pudgy *tommes,* as big around as small pizzas, pleasing in thickness and heft. Régine carved the date into the side of each using a penlike tool with a small loop of wire at one end instead of a nib. The cheeses also carried a green casein label, meaning they were *mixte*—i.e., made from both sheep's and cow's milk. Though the Pyrenees are known for *brebis,* lots of farms have long kept a few cows, and the Miramons have ten. (The cows happened to be Holsteins, but Régine was quick to say they wanted to change the herd over to Montbéliardes, which, though an Alpine breed, is at least French.) Sheep, you will recall, give a lot less milk than cows, so a farmer can stretch his sheep's milk by mixing a few cows into the herd and making *tomme mixte.* In the days before labels, the *tommes* were marked with metal stamps pressed into the cheeses—an O for sheep (or *ovin*), an *I* for cow's milk, and an *I* traced over an O for a *tomme mixte.* The marks looked more like runes than letters, as though the cheeses were meant for some now forgotten pagan ritual.

Turning aside from the previous day's rounds, Régine set about the morning's work: making straight-up *tomme de brebis.* I watched her attach blades to the rotor arm over her vat. She hit a switch and the machine whirled, cutting the firmed curd into grains that would release more whey. Once the curd was cut, she suctioned most of the whey off with a silver tube, revealing ivory, jujube-size bits already clumping together, ready to be chunked into molds. After she had them portioned out, she stacked the overflowing molds into a press, essentially an open stainless-steel rectangle, and lowered a hydraulic arm to start the pressing.

As she bent to encrust the cheeses from the day before in glittery white grains of salt—this she did by hand even though the salt left her skin raw and red—she started telling me about the high pastures. "Up there they don't have any of this, of course. When René makes his cheeses, he pierces the curd with long needles to release the whey and presses them by hand." She looked at me. "He's a true shepherd"—her expression grew wry—"and a real character." René had taught Régine much of what she knew about cheesemaking. She pulled out a book titled *Estives,* which had been published in a nearby town. The cover showed a precipice, below which grazed the tiny white forms of sheep. In profile, a lone man leaned on a walking stick, one foot poised on a rock as he gazed over them. The man, she told me, was René.

Once they are made, Régine sends her cheeses away for aging in a former railway tunnel. Then they're returned to the Miramons, who keep a small storefront in town. As she finished with the morning's tasks, Régine offered to show me the shop. I'd seen it on my way through town, a portion of building along the highway that had been painted a tangerine orange; it stood out from the rest of Bedous's somber buildings as well as if it had been outlined in neon.

The shop's lime-green inside turned out to be as bright as its outside. Régine's mother-in-law, a cushiony woman in a sweater and floral skirt, chatted with a customer near the cash register. Meanwhile Régine bustled about, cutting hunks of different cheeses for me: a three-month-old *mixte* and a five-month-old *brebis.* For dinner the night before, Jean-Claude at the bed-and-breakfast had suggested a small restaurant on Bedous's main drag. They'd served me a lovely meal, followed by slices of the Miramons' *tomme*—whether *brebis* or *mixte,* the woman at the restaurant hadn't been quite sure. I told Régine this and she frowned slightly in surprise. "She didn't know?" she said. "Hmmm. It was *mixte.* Cow's milk makes the *mixte* creamier," she explained. Pure *brebis* also takes longer to mature, with the result that the *fromage* is noticeably drier—flaky, with a parmesan-like texture that almost crumbles in your mouth.

As for taste—trying to explain the difference between other cheeses and a *fromage* that contains sheep's milk is a lot like trying to explain the difference between a cheese made of cow's milk and one made of goat's milk. Once you've had a *chèvre,* you know that taste—the particular tang that says "goat." Sheep's-milk cheese has its own particular note, too; the chic cheese-taster word for it is *lanolin.* Once you've eaten one, you can identify the taste, but it's tough to put the difference into words, other than to say a *brebis* tastes, well, sheep-y. As the cheese ages, the flavor can get quite sharp, the reason that, in some places, such as the Basque Country, the traditional pairing for such cheeses is black cherry jam. Besides tasting of sheep, *brebis* often reminds me of roasted almonds—the richest, best roasted almonds you've ever tasted combined with hints of sweet mountain grasses.

The shop walls were decorated with photographs of the Miramons' *estive.* Régine showed me an old photo of René, a stump of a man who somehow looked already gnarled next to a younger and slimmer version of his wife. Behind them stood a solid stone-and-mortar *cabane*—a shepherd's hut—roofed in sheet metal, with solar panels in the rear. A line of propane tanks leaned against one wall, before a backdrop of silver milk jugs, sheep, and rocky outcroppings. In another image, a herd of Basco-Béarnaise sat in picturesque splendor, the long curls of their white fleeces looking like dreadlocks. In one close-up, a sheep wore a bell longer than its own long face.

The day before, I'd driven down the *nationale* farther into the valley, where clusters of houses clung to the mountainsides, hamlets so slight they seemed like scenes from a pop-up book of children's tales; I half expected them to fold back into their scrap of plateau as soon as I went around the next bend. Up there somewhere during the summer months, the shepherds perch. Getting to the Miramons' *estive,* according to Régine, took about half an hour by car and then two or three more hours on foot. I thought wistfully of going, knowing it was impossible. Even though purple blooms of wisteria already scented the air in town, the route up to the *estive* would still be covered in snow. But I'd asked to meet René, and Régine told me to report back later that afternoon. Before leaving, I motioned to a picture on the wall in which the slightly bowlegged form of René, cigarette dangling from his mouth, led a pack mule. "Is that how they get the cheeses off the mountain at the end of the season?" I asked. "Actually," Régine said, "they use helicopters."

IN PERSON, René Miramon was even stumpier and more dwarf-like than in the photos. He wore a grubby plaid shirt, a green cardigan, and a pair of dark denim jeans. His skin looked permanently raw from summer after summer spent in too-thin air; a slash of scarlet marked the bridge of his nose, and more redness scored his cheeks. White chest hair peeked from beneath an undershirt, and he'd tucked a pouch of tobacco into one pocket. But at sixty-six, he had a full head of hair, with only patches of gray, and his eyes were dark and alert. He spoke a French that sounded as though it had been influenced heavily by Spanish: thick, with a rolling, rounded accent like clotted cream.

While waiting for five o'clock to arrive, I'd located the one shop in town that sold books, and purchased a copy of *Estives,* the coffee-table book with the picture of René on the cover. I sat across from him at the dining table in his house, adjacent to the cheese shop, and offered him the book. The pages are stuffed with photos accompanied only by such unilluminating captions as "Looking for strays." At the beginning of the book, René is identified as *"le solitaire de Banassole."* I asked him what this meant, wondering why he was described as the "lone man" of Banassole. He answered that Banassole was his "sector" of the mountains, his grazing lands. It was, he said, 2,000 meters (6,561 feet) up. He began turning pages. "Wait," he said. "I have to get my glasses." As he sat back down at the table, a pair of wire-rimmed spectacles in hand, he had me pull my ladder-backed wooden chair next to his own, then began turning pages again, pointing to the different mountain chains and rattling off names. "Here, you see, Banassole is located on this peak here, and then there is another mountain chain, because there are two mountain chains, and this is the range on the other side, which is over there, and this one here is another range, that goes into Spain, as far as Somport, if you like."

Apparently not satisfied that I'd truly gotten the lay of the land, he shifted, chair creaking, and said, "I'll try to make you understand another way." He flipped more pages, stopping only to make comments such as "This is this mountain range that goes toward the border, then turns and comes back into France, and this range here goes this way, and this peak is here . . ." When he paused, I threw out questions, hoping for more than a speedy topography lesson. He paid me no mind. After nearly fifteen minutes of peak-naming and page-turning, we stopped on a picture and he said, "My *cabane* is behind over there," motioning to an area outside the frame.

"What's life like up there?" I put in. "Could you describe it?"

He looked at me. "Nah," he said.

I blinked. "Wow," I said finally, "you really know your mountains."

Eventually, as he flipped and paged, a picture of life in the *estive* emerged in snippets. When René was younger, he would leave for the high pastures on a midsummer's night, walking pack animals and moon-bright sheep through the darkness to avoid traffic on the road. The following morning, they'd arrive at the *cabane*. When the book's photographer came around in the early 2000s, there were two other shepherds working with René. By the time he and I spoke some half dozen years later, he'd spent a number of seasons alone. Nearly every man pictured in *Estives* looked as weather-beaten as René himself. As he pointed at various figures, he told me, "This one is dead now, and that one, he's dead, too."

As you might already guess, life in the *estive* was much harder when René was still a young man. "Look," he said, showing me a stunted *cabane,* bits of junk piled against unmortared walls of stone, a rusted skin of metal for the roof. An overturned pail lay forgotten in one corner. "The living conditions were impossible. Impossible! The *cabanes* we have now are no more than twenty-five years old. But before that, look, look." He prodded the glossy image with a blunt finger. "Imagine, can you, what that was like when it was cold, when the wind blew, when it rained? And back then there was no gas. No heat, no way to cook except for over a wood fire—and you had to go a long way to find wood." Men came with pack mules every ten days or so to bring fresh supplies up and take cheeses down. I asked how many cheeses one mule could carry. René mulled it over. "Eight," he offered. In a typical summer, he might make one hundred cheeses.

"So it took some time," I said, "to get them all down."

René punctuated my comments with short, sharp, groaning wails. "And don't forget," he said, "the supply men must be paid!"

Supply men still make the rounds of the *estives* every few weeks with fresh produce, fruit, and news from the valley below. In addition, there are now also radios, solar panels, lights, propane tanks—and of course the helicopters, which are subsidized by the French government. Each *berger* gets to send a packet of supplies up on the chopper at the beginning of the season; the helicopter returns in the fall to bring the supplies and finished cheeses down.

"They've helped us, and we've evolved," René said, "but fifteen years too late, and maybe even twenty years too late. The young people are gone. They got discouraged and left." I asked how many shepherds remained, sending him off into a round of counting: "And on that mountain, there's one, no two, *bergers*." I tallied until he reached forty-five shepherds on the peaks surrounding the valley. Of these, he thought perhaps seven were in their thirties or forties; one was a daughter rather than a son. Each *estive* averaged one or two. "There used to be six or seven on each mountain," he said. "It's not like it was."

René's new companions are tourists—loads of hikers who come to see him so often that he complained it was sometimes hard to get the cheeses made. The tourists come, of course, because even with the helicopters and the comfort of propane tanks, René and his fellow Pyrenees *fromagers* haven't modernized in other ways. The tourists come to see René press his cheeses in the old stainless-steel molds he insists on using instead of the modern molds of white plastic others use, molds which René says "make a cheese that looks too much like a factory cheese." The tourists come to see a cheesemaking *à la main* from start to finish, just as it's always been. They come to see him milk his sheep by hand.

• • •

IT'S A LOVELY story, made even lovelier because in this instance it's true. It is not, however, a story without costs—take those expensive government-subsidized helicopters. Government aid has been a fixture of European farming since the 1960s, when the sting of wartime food shortages was still fresh. The European Communities (a forerunner to the European Union) set up the Common Agricultural Policy (CAP), a Europe-wide system of agricultural subsidies aimed at augmenting production. The program succeeded a little too well: the "butter mountains" and "wine lakes" that resulted are the stuff of legend. To bring supply back in line with demand, the member countries instituted quotas—among them the 1984 milk quota, which penalizes dairy farmers if they produce beyond a certain set limit, along with a series of subsequent reforms, a number of them aimed at promoting a more free-market approach.

Despite these measures, the CAP continues to account for a jumbo portion of the European Union's budget—a few years ago spending was close to €53 billion, or $72 billion—four times what the United States spends, and nearly half the European Union's total expenditures. French farmers, cheese-makers among them, receive direct-payment subsidies, which range from very small payments of a few hundred euros to tens of thousands of euros per year and occasionally more. Critics complain about inefficiency and the questionable distribution of CAP dollars; until recently, where those dollars actually went was a "state secret." New disclosure laws, however, revealed that

85 percent of aid goes to a 17 percent sliver of large agrobusiness firms and privileged landowners. Among them are the Queen of England, who in 2008 got $778,812 for Sandringham Estate, a twenty-thousand-acre royal retreat, and Prince Albert of Monaco, recipient of over half a million dollars for his French wheat farms.

In response, food producers, especially the French ones, point to all they do, much of it uncompensated, to maintain the *terroir* everyone so loves. European consumers, these producers remind opponents, have demanded environmentally responsible farming methods, an expensive constraint their global competitors do not face. Jean-Louis Miramon, for one, made a point of telling me during a pause in my barn tour with Régine that they didn't allow genetically modified organisms in their cow and sheep feed. "You know, Monsanto," he'd said, looking up from the yogurt he was eating to wave an admonishing spoon in my direction.

Discontinuing farm subsidies would probably put artisanal cheese beyond the budgets of many. Then again, even with subsidies, traditional French cheeses (and in the United States, "new" artisanal cheeses made on French models) are unquestionably luxury products—very tasty niche items sought out by a small percentage of the population.

And luxury relies on a good story, usually a tale of how difficult it was to make or procure something. No matter how genuine they are in their dedication to tradition, *affineurs* such as Hervé Mons know this quite well. Hearing about expense affects us in a way that can be measured empirically: studies have found that if we are told that something, a wine perhaps, is more expensive, the part of our brain that registers pleasure becomes more active. We all like to hear about the guy who wakes up at 4:00 A.M. every day to milk his cows by hand and then make cheese in a big wooden bucket. There is something about the thought of all that labor—of a human bringing something into the world by sheer dint of muscle—that we value. Hence the struggle over cheesemakers' use of technology, and the sense that making cheese with the help of laborsaving devices is somehow cheating.

Nevertheless, even with a few portable milking machines, making Salers in a *buron* (or Camembert in a farmhouse, or *tomme de pays* on a Pyrenean mountaintop) continues to require staggering amounts of unrelenting physical work. That much had been obvious as I stood inside Guy Chambon's *buron* that morning in Auvergne, watching the moisture sheening his brow as he helped Julien, the summer hand, wrestle two barrelsful of milk off a hand truck and into his cheesemaking room. The barrels, called *gerles,* are made of wood and come up to mid-thigh, with a circumference about a foot and a half across; they're just big enough that you could dunk yourself in them. Smaller, not to mention lighter, containers might have been easier, but solid chestnut wood is traditional—and essential to making the cheese properly. In the mid-2000s there was an attempt by EU health officials to ban the *gerles,* amid worries that they were unsanitary. But the Salers producers rebelled, insisting that the barrels posed no risk. They were correct: subsequent research proved that the wood actually protects against contamination by promoting the growth of good bacteria. This, unfortunately, doesn't make the *gerles* any less heavy. When the time came to begin making cheese, Guy dipped out as much of the whey as he could, then he and Julien each took a side in order to tip the curds into a shallow, rectangular stainless-steel trough.

This was the pressing table. If you're making a larger cheese in a place with lots of trees, you can, of course, "cook" the curd to expel more whey and then press it, as they used to do in the old days with Beaufort. But if you're pasturing your cows in a place with few trees, you have to resort to other, somewhat more drastic methods, and this was where the pressing table came in. Julien had helped Guy prep the table by draping it in a linen cloth moistened with whey. Now Guy folded the sides of the cloth over the heaping mound of curd, wrapping it well. He lowered a ladder-shaped grating over the top of the curd, winching it closed with a chain-link rope. After a few minutes, he removed the lid and unwrapped the linen to reveal a big, rectangular block of smooshed-together curd. He cut the block into smaller pieces, stacked these one on top of the other in the center of the press, rewrapped them, and brought the lid down again. Over the next few hours, he would repeat this process—known as "cheddaring" because it's also used to make that cheese—a dozen times, working slowly and methodically to remove more and more whey.

At the end of all this pressing and cutting, Guy ended up with what's known as *tomme fraîche*—"fresh tomme"—a springy, thick cake of curd that resembles a big piece of a foam mattress. *Tomme fraîche* figures large in the traditional peasant fare of the Massif Central, in dishes such as *aligot,* in which the *tomme* is whipped with potatoes, butter, garlic, and whatever else the cook thinks might taste good in the mix. Usually *aligot* is shown being pulled upward on a large spoon as if it were saltwater taffy, an image that might as well be patented for the dish; if you see a picture of some Frenchy, creamy, cheesy-looking thing being stretched on a wooden utensil, you can bet it's *aligot.* And not only does it look like glue, but it *is* like glue. It's difficult to imagine how this can possibly taste good, but it does: I once ate so much I had to nearly roll myself out of my chair afterward. It was worth every sticky, stretchy mouthful.

Given the rest of the Salers-making process, you can see why people would have wanted to stop with the *tomme fraîche.* Because if you're going to keep going and make Salers, you next have to let the *tomme* "repose" for about twenty hours. While Guy worked, Julien took out a big block of *tomme fraîche* from the day before, cut it in half, and placed it in a stainless-steel tub with another waiting *tomme.* While the *tomme* from that morning's milking continued to press in the table, Guy turned to the day-old *tomme,* cutting it into smaller hunks, which he set next to what looked like a meat grinder. He dumped a few hunks into the grinder's stainless-steel basket and took hold of the handle. Then he began to crank. This *broyage*—"grinding"—makes the texture of the finished cheese somewhat friable. Auvergne's proximity to ancient salt routes greatly influenced the recipe for *fourmes*, and Guy added copious amounts of salt to the pellet-sized grains that spewed into a catch basin.

Only at the end of this whole process could Guy finally mold up his cheeses. It was a morning of cheesemaking that contained manual task after manual task after manual task. Droplets of sweat dripped from the end of Guy's nose as he ground the *tomme*, and he would pause periodically in order to "rest" by changing the cloths and turning the cheeses he had molded the day before. The cheesemaking room was smallish and square, with white-tiled walls. The stained beige floor had a drain in the middle as if it were a giant shower stall. And it felt like a shower: close and damp. I was exhausted just standing there watching him.

NO DOUBT THERE will always be cheesemakers such as Guy, individuals determined to do it the hard way, people for whom the older ways of life still call, no matter the obstacles. In the early 1980s, Guy's *buron* was destroyed when a huge storm with exceptionally high winds ravaged ten million square meters of the Auvergne countryside. For twenty years the place sat in ruin. But, Guy said, "I rebuilt." When I asked why, he said he'd missed it.

Begrudging him his one small modernization devalues everything else he does. And it overlooks the truth that cheese not only makes use of science and technology, it *is* science and technology. It has been since the days when ancient peoples first filled calves' stomachs with milk and then poured the resulting curd into a basket specially woven for the job. "A living tradition," writes French cheese historian Pierre Boisard, "is not something frozen for all time, not something perfectly defined or hemmed in by immutable rules," nor is it "some absolute respect for a mythical past." There are makers who use the past as a guide—who respect the past, but who don't hesitate to move forward, who know that one need not necessarily contradict the other. In spite of Régine's and Jean-Louis's very modern cheesemaking facility in the valley, their sheep go to the mountains in the summers—and they will continue to go. When I asked René if he would go to the *estive* that summer, he said no. He was too old; it was getting to be too much. Jean-Louis would go. I wondered aloud if Jean-Louis wanted to go, and René looked at me, considering. "Listen," he said, and gave an abrupt chuckle. "*C'est son métier.*" Jean-Louis would go and live in the *cabane,* milk his sheep by hand, and make his cheese the same way because that is what a *berger* does.

René may be a crusty old shepherd, but he is one who nonetheless knows that clinging to the thing we no longer have is what Buddhists would call suffering. "People want to live the way other people live; they don't want such labor-intensive work. No one moves anymore," René said to me as we finished our talk. "No one walks. They all have cars. When I was young, we didn't go to school like they do now. And my parents were farmers. There was little choice." Then he shrugged. "But that's the evolution of our society," he said. *"Et c'est normal."* That's as it should be.

CODA: JOYEUSES
CHEESE FÊTES

~~~~~~~~~~

"Cheese is the biscuit of drunkards."

—GRIMOD DE LA REYNIÈRE

Trumpets blare, a sound both glad and bold, as a line of green-caped people marches solemnly by twos through a stone archway in the sixteenth-century Tower of Navarre in the town of Langres. In addition to the cape, which is trimmed and lined in gold, a golden medal shines from each chest, and every head bears a tricorn hat. They sweep in an arch before the camera, the wooden staves they carry clicking the floor now and again, to pool behind a table draped in a forest-green cloth, bare save for a dozen or so packaged *fromages de Langres* piled in an artful pyramid. A man steps forward and holds out his stave, shorter than the others and decoratively carved, a few feet above the middle of the table. He opens his hand, allowing the stave to fall with a resounding thwack before calling for the cheese knights to doff their hats.

One of the members introduces him: "The Grand Maître of the Navarre Tower of Langres, Eric, speaks!" (In order to get the full effect, you have to imagine the name as it is pronounced in French: Errr-RIK!) Eric begins, saying, "In this year of grace two thousand and seven of our current era [. . .] in the presence of the good people, the dignitaries, the *chevaliers* and the brotherhood, I, Eric de Langres, declare open the twenty-fifth chapter of the Confrérie des Tastes-Fromages de Langres." A knight intones, "Let the cheese be brought forth!" and a green-caped woman steps forward bearing a straw tray. Eric takes a slice as the knight queries: "Does it please the Grand Maître to taste the *fromage,* conceived in the tradition of good living?"

"It pleases me," Eric replies, bestowing a beneficent glance upon the assembly before taking a bite. He chews. The camera cuts to the woman making the rounds with the tray, offering a sliver to each person as though it were a communion wafer. Everyone chews. The camera swings back to Eric.

"*Ma foi*"—my goodness—"this cheese is worthy of our palates and your tables. I confer and confirm its title of Fromage de Langres!"

THESE SCENES FROM this elaborate twenty-fifth-anniversary gathering of the Confrérie des Tastes-Fromages de Langres were captured for a short film, *Tout un fromage de Langres,* which was among the spoils conferred on me by Eric de Langres (aka Eric Masselier), deputy mayor of Langres by day, Grand Maître of the Confrérie by night. Though the Elks may not exist in France, and you won't find any Shriner temples, the presence of *confréries* means that the ordinary French person does not lack for opportunities to don a funny hat and join with others to eat, drink, and perform selfless acts. These "brotherhoods"— nowadays there are also a lot of *consœurs,* or "co-sisters," who join the "co-brothers"—exist for all sorts of interests, not just gastronomic ones, but the ones dedicated to food and drink are particularly lively. There is, for example, a Confrérie de la Moutarde de Dijon, a Confrérie des Macarons, and a Confrérie du Pâté de Foie, as well as groups dedicated to The Turkey of Licques, The Oysters of la Baie, The Onion of Auxonne, and The Cauliflower of Saint-Omer. And while the largest number of *confréries* (246) is clustered about wines and champagnes, at least twenty are devoted to *fromage.* The granddaddy of these is the Confrérie des Chevaliers du Taste-Fromage, founded in Paris by Pierre Androuët, whose members embrace all French cheeses. Others are dedicated to a single, lucky *fromage.*

As far as the French are concerned, the *confréries* are among the most solemn and important of cheese institutions—and only the most worthy of foreigners are invited to join. In *French Lessons: Adventures with Knife, Fork, and Corkscrew,* author Peter Mayle attends the Fattest Eater speed-eating contest in Livarot because a journalist friend (who'd written glowingly of the town's cheese) is being inducted into the Confrérie des Chevaliers du Fromage de Livarot during the festival. "It's the cheese hall of fame," the friend explains. "I'm getting a medal. The town will spend the whole weekend celebrating. The streets will be running with wine and Livarot." In the PBS documentary about her research into French cheese, Mother Noëlla Marcellino, the Cheese Nun, also gets inducted into a local *confrérie*. She's hard put not to burst into tears when they knight her.

The Grand Master also gave me a book on Langres and a green-and-gold lapel pin depicting the badge of the *confrérie*. I'd driven through a sugarplum dusting of early December snow to reach Langres, which lies to the southeast of Paris. The Navarre Tower and the other various towers and gates that punctuate the ramparts of the fortified village are situated on the Langres Plateau, an elevated piece of land surrounded by rolling pastures that gleamed greenly through the melting whiteness. From those fertile swathes came the *fromages,* which were originally made by farmwives; unlike so many rind-washed types, the history of Langres is entirely monk-free. The already tiny production had a brush with death after World War I, when the cheese almost disappeared. Today it has rebounded somewhat, with four producers, one of whom is *fermier.* "It's one of the smallest AOC productions," Eric said. "It's a relatively little-known cheese."

In person, Eric was affable and fiftyish, with a slightly ruddy face that hinted at mischief. He wore a corduroy jacket over a gray turtleneck and carried a well-worn leather briefcase. We sat chatting at a table in the mayor's office, where he showed me several pictures of the *confrérie,* the members outfitted in their capes and hats.

"Why the outfits?" I asked.

"Awww," he said, amused. "Why the outfits, why the outfits? Because they're the distinctive sign of the brotherhood." He began explaining how the system worked. "There are three ranks: the *Membres d'Honneur,* the *Chevaliers d'Honneur,* and the *Chevaliers de Cape.*" The Honorary Members, who are numerous and can have attended as few as one event, get a shiny Langres medal with a gold chain; the Knights of Honor, one rank up, have medals with ribbons; and the Knights of the Cape earn their snazzy green cape after proving their devotion to the *confrérie* by attending five or so events a year for several years. The colors of the brotherhood's robes signify the "green of the prairies" and the "yellow of the cheese." They also happen to be the exact shades of green and gold used by the Green Bay Packers football franchise. It seemed I was coming full circle in my cheese wanderings.

The Grand Maître des Tastes Fromages de Langres is elected by a governing committee, and holds the office for as long as he's willing, "or until they throw me out," Eric said. The mission of the *confrérie,* he explained, was to "promote always and everywhere the cheese of the good village of Langres and the *pays* of Langres"—this is the oath they swear. "For example," he explained, "every year there's an automobile rally in Langres that brings in people from across France. We go down in our costumes and have them *déguster* the *fromage*. They usually leave with some cheese." Just the previous weekend, several members had gone to Italy, morsels of Langres at the ready. And the brotherhood had worked hard to help the cheese get its AOC. "It's to promote a product that one esteems to be of quality, which gives satisfaction to epicureans." He paused. "You know what an epicurean is, right?" I assured him I was familiar with the term. "Good things," he continued, fixing me with one eye, "pretty women, the good life."

"And good cheese," I prompted.

"Of course!" he said, hastening to add that he'd made a point of increasing the *confrérie*'s female membership—now at about 40 percent—and was also working on trying to induce young people to join. "You have to have time, and a little bit of money" to partake, he said, which meant that most of the *chevaliers* were over fifty.

"Can you describe how a good Langres tastes?" I said.

"Hah!" he said. "I can't tell you that because naturally it's the best cheese there is!" He laughed. "No, no, I like all the cheeses of France, but I do always have Langres on the cheese platter for my guests." Back in the old days, Eric said, Langres's goldeny-orange hue came from aging, but now that the aging period is shorter, they brush the rind with annatto, a natural colorant made from the pods of a bush found in the Americas. Besides the vivid annatto coloring, Langres is the only French cheese with a sunken top. As the moist curd sticks to the sides of the

cylindrical molds used to make them, the center of the top col-
lapses, making the larger cheeses look like fallen cakes, while
the smaller specimens resemble oversize caramels. According
to Rance, the indent in the top allows brine to pool and then
sink during aging, making for a sublimely rich finished cheese.
It's also a handy receptacle for spirits: you can fill the well with
champagne or brandy to create a glorious cheese-pie mess of
alcohol-laced *fromage*.

One of the events the organization puts on to promote the
cheese, Eric told me, is a *goûtaillon*.

"A *goûtaillon*?" I asked. "Is that a *dégustation*?"

He shook his head. "It's better." Four times a year they find
a chef willing to accept the challenge of creating a meal around
the *fromage*. By secret ballot, the members score the main dish,
which must somehow incorporate Langres. If the chef scores
high enough, he's automatically inducted into the brotherhood.
The next *goûtaillon*, as chance would have it, was set to take place
just two days hence.

Unfortunately, I was scheduled to leave the following day for
the region of Brie. So I made my good-byes to Eric and set off
back to the guesthouse where I was staying. Along the way, I
thought about Brie. Then I thought about Langres. I thought
about the *goûtaillon*. I thought about the fact that, genial though
he was, Eric hadn't invited me to the dinner. Maybe it was a
members-only kind of thing? Probably it would be rude to in-
vite myself. It didn't matter. I already had reservations in Brie.

The following morning, I sat in my car and looked at my

phone, considering. I punched in Eric's number. "Ah, about that *goûtaillon*," I said. "Do you think I could come?"

He paused for half a second. "Gladly, we'd love to have you." I let out a whoop as I hung up the phone. Yes! Forget Brie. I was going to a stinky-cheese shindig.

AS I MADE my way to the back room of the restaurant in Langres that was hosting the *goûtaillon,* it was obvious that word of an American *journaliste* had preceded me. A clot of people stood in the entryway, all of whom shook my hand and said, "*Bonsoir, Madame,*" and none of whom wore a "Who the hell are you?" look. One of the *Chevaliers de Cape* came up to chat, and when I gave him my name, he said, "*Oh, c'est vous?*" I asked where they'd come up with the word *goûtaillon*—which is not actually a word in French. He said it was Eric's doing. Put together *goût* and *cotillion,* and you get the idea. It's a cheese-tasting debutante ball.

Thirty or so *confrères* and *consœurs* milled about tables arrayed in smart monochromatic leaf-patterned linens and beautifully set with stemware and white plates. The walls were painted a vibrant persimmon, and a garland of shiny Christmas packages framed a doorway leading to the main seating area. Eric greeted me warmly, addressing me with the informal *tu,* and the *soirée* was off. He had seated me to his right, sandwiched between him and the mayor of Langres, using place cards—apparently not a usual *goûtaillon* device. "He's got some funny ideas," the bespectacled woman across from me groused. "I was better over there." She waved her hand toward the chair she'd been blithely occupying before someone pointed out the cards to her, and refused to look at me. She later warmed as she recounted a five-week road trip she'd once made across the United States. Once the wine got going, she eventually confided that she was actually a Parisian, and preferred Paris to Langres. But it was a secret; I shouldn't tell anyone.

Before the meal got under way, Eric stood to address his knights. He welcomed everyone and began explaining that there were several special guests that night, including the mayor and an American writer. Dread washed over me as I realized what was coming: he was going to make me say a few words. Nothing like an impromptu speech in a foreign language to start off an evening. "And now," he said, "I'll let Kathe Lison, who joins us from the United States, explain her project." I can't remember what I said precisely, though it included something about researching "*la vie fromagère,*" at which point I had to stop and ask "if you can say that in French?" To which Eric replied, "Not really, but we get it." I retook my seat with some relief as the serving got under way. Two unlit Christmas candles dotted the tables near us. I lit a snowman, and Eric lit a Christmas tree, then nestled it among my stemware. Consolation for putting me on the spot.

Kitty-corner to me sat a Danish couple who'd retired to Langres a handful of years earlier—a pretty blonde and her husband, a jovial man with a large, brushlike mustache. An even more impressive mustache covered the mayor's upper lip, and by the time we'd worked through the first course—a lettuce salad with warm chopped ham accompanied by a Chinese egg and slices of baguette topped with melted Langres—the two had dubbed themselves *les confrères moustachus* and were clinking glasses. Eric, meanwhile, explained about the scorecards laid out by each place setting. "You have found the Specialty," each prompted, followed by a twenty-point scale with descriptors ranging from *quelconque*—"mediocre"—to *délicieuse*. Anything below eight was considered "Mac Doh," though when I later verified the "Mac Doh" rating with Eric, he said, "No, no, don't put that in!" and changed it to "*le fast food.*" I said it was okay, even Americans are aware Mac Doh isn't exactly haute cuisine. There was no perfect score because, *bien sûr,* "in cooking, there is no perfection." The chef's main dish had to score at least 14 out of 20 to earn him induction into the brotherhood. The former *Parisienne* across the table informed me that the *confrérie* didn't limit itself to dining in Langres—the group had been known to range as far away as Dijon, about an hour to the south, to find chefs who were willing to put their cheese-cooking powers to the test.

As we sipped wine and waited for the main course to arrive, the mayor launched into a disquisition on the number of international visitors who had come inquiring about *fromages de Langres,* calling on Eric to help: "And there was that Canadian woman, remember, what was her name again?" Finally, they established that the order claimed members not only in Quebec, but also

Japan, Ireland, and several other European countries. On his placemat, the mayor drew an impromptu schematic, scribbling little circles in very rough geographical approximation and labeling them. (Under "U.S.A.," he wrote, "Wisconsin, Kathe Lison.") "We should pull together an international gathering, hey, Eric?" he said, and drew a hexagon into which he placed another circle labeled "Langres." While the mayor's plans for this Langres Cheese Summit grew ever more grandiose, Eric— clearly considering logistical difficulties rather than rosy images of peoples the world over coming together in cheese harmony— grunted in reply and avoided the mayor's eye.

The main course arrived: a chicken thigh and leg smothered in a *sauce Langres,* flanked by a concoction of baked egg and zucchini and a side of woefully overcooked vegetables. I took a bite of the chicken. Not great. The sauce made with the Langres, on the other hand, was fantastic: maybe I was swayed by the orange color of the cheese, but there was something almost carrot-y about its deep salty sweetness that nearly rescued the lackluster poultry.

"What do you think?" Eric asked.

"*Elle est bonne, la sauce,*" I offered.

He nodded and leaned in to say, "Langres is the king of cheeses, you know." The next course, a small salad with Langres-filled *gougères,* was terrific. Give me a cheese-filled pastry and I'm there. The conversation turned to the difficulty of luring good chefs to a small town such as Langres, and the mayor, an extremely slender man, complained that no one in Paris really enjoyed eating anymore. Everyone's rail thin, he said, everyone's on a diet. But in the countryside, they still knew how to eat. We enthusiastically proved his point by downing the warm apple compote and ice cream served for dessert.

By this time the room glowed softly with the mélange of food, Langres, and wine—bottles of both red and white having moved along the tables with splendid alacrity. Once the plates had been cleared, all attention turned to scoring. Not wanting to be rude and scuttle the chef's average, I hesitated. "What are you going to put?" I whispered to the mayor.

"Ah," he shrugged, "it's a twelve out of twenty." That was good enough for me, and I marked the box next to "*Bonne.*" Someone gathered the ballots for tallying. Then Eric moved to the head of the room, donned his Grand Maître medal, set his tricorn hat on his head at a rakish angle, and took up his polished shepherd's stave. He began by leading the assembly in a spirited rendition of the *confrérie*'s song:

> *A well-ripened Langres, and my worries are far away,*
> *With a glass of claret, my heart rejoices*
> *At six o'clock, at noon, or when the day closes*
> *I savor my fromage by singing this adage:*
> *Lingonese formaticum, formaticum lingonese*

As the last lines died away, people cheered. Then the honors commenced, with a *chevalier* who had earned a "Langres d'Or," a special medallion mounted on a green background and framed in gilt, given every two years for outstanding service to the order. Eric reminded the knights that anyone could earn the coveted Langres d'Or, and without limit: one could earn two or three, or even four! It was easy to see why he'd been made Grand Maître. He played the role with seriousness combined with a whiff of tongue-in-cheek, while managing somehow to avoid tilting into full-blown farce. He continued with another award, retaining the correct air of pomp even as "Wake Me Up Before You Go-Go" by Wham! began playing on the restaurant's sound system.

"Though it wasn't foreseen," I heard him say, "and it's quite rare—that must be underlined—I think you will agree that I don't bend the rules often. So, as an exception—and because this is, after all, a gathering of exceptional people, I ask Madame Kathe Lison to join me." Next to me, the mayor let out a belly chuckle, and people began to clap. I staggered to my feet and wobbled to the front of the room—I'd had a lot of wine—to stand in front of Eric, Grand Maître des Tastes Fromages de Langres. "*Ma chère* Kathe," he said, "I am very happy that you are here. We haven't known each other for very long, but I hope that this visit is only the first of many. This is for you." And he produced a shiny golden medal with a golden chain, the medal of the *confrérie*. Shouts of "Ho!" went up from the assembled *chevaliers* while I tried to contain my startled glee. Then the medal was somehow hanging around my neck as Eric dubbed me a

Membre d'Honneur de la Confrérie des Tastes-Fromages de Langres with all the obligations, rights, and privileges thereof.

As he went through the ritual, I felt both moved and silly. I didn't know what to do with my hands. They were at my sides, clasped in front of me, clasped over my heart. Maybe I should cry? Afterward, I examined my medal—which turned out to be ceramic—and showed it off to the Danish couple and the mayor. The back was signed "Eric de Langres," with the date. The mayor named each of the structures on the medal's device: the cathedral, the Tower of Navarre, the Langres main city gate. "I wasn't expecting that," I said to the mayor. I blinked, realizing I'd become rather dewy-eyed. The mayor's lips quirked with amusement as he gave me a sideways glance over his huge mustache. But that was okay. I'd been made a cheese knight.

In a few weeks I would be in Paris, with Chris, where we would share our long-awaited Mont d'Or—a billowy, spruce-banded round almost exactly like the one we'd smuggled home in our suitcase years before. On Christmas night we broke into the rind and licked the *pâte* from the backs of our spoons. The cheese was succulent, assertive, and strong, tasting powerfully of cow, with the texture of a runny Brie—like eating the richest white chocolate imaginable, only with salt instead of sugar. Sitting in the City of Light, eating that *fromage*—it was a long way from the trailer in which I'd first learned to love cheese by making boxed Kraft macaroni with my mother. But as we ate, we would talk not so much of Paris, nor even of the cheese (though

Chris was relieved the Mont d'Or did not, as he'd feared, taste like Chuck Taylor sneakers), but of home. This, perhaps, is the true power and mystique of cheese: how it feeds not just the body, but the soul; how, even in the most faraway places, it can bring you back home.

As the evening in Langres wound down, the chef was awarded his medal: he'd scored a respectable 14 out of 20, good enough for "*très bonne*" and induction into the *confrérie*. And then, too soon, the festivities were over. With many kisses, I took my leave of my new friends. As I tottered off toward my bed, I felt besotted by more than just the wine. We had only just met, but in the space of one evening, brought together by nothing more than spoiled milk, I'd found a place and a people in the world I could come back to. A place where I would be greeted with open arms, where my cheese brothers and sisters would take me in and feed me up on *fromage,* if ever I needed it. A place that felt, at least a little, like home.

I walked through the chill of the December night below loops of twinkly lights strung on wires above the street. White bulbs outlined stars and the words *Joyeuses Fêtes.* Happy Holidays, indeed.

ACKNOWLEDGMENTS

My heartfelt thanks to everyone who helped make this a much better book than it would otherwise have been. You know who you are, and that I could not have done it without you.

Et aux fromagères et fromagers de France—et à toutes les personnes de la filière du fromage, qui m'ont accueillie avec tant de générosité— j'adresse mes plus sincères remerciements. Ce livre n'aurait pu voir le jour sans vous.

SELECTED PARISIAN *FROMAGERIES*

Few things can beat heading into the French countryside to buy fresh local cheeses sold at some village *marché*. However, when such forays aren't possible, Paris isn't exactly a bad option. Here, then, is a list of some favorite cheese stores in the city.

Androuët: Though you can still walk along rue d'Amsterdam, and find the number 41 emblazoned on a stone crest flanked by two cherubic children, the store's old medieval façade is gone—replaced (at least when I was there) by modish panes of frosted apple-green glass, all right angles and sans serif fonts, that advertise new wares in English: "cookies, salad bar, and smoothies." After going through some rough years, Pierre Androuët sold the business to a conglomerate in the late 1980s, an act that subjected him to some derision. Pierre's daughter, Isabelle, assures me that the seven locations around the city are now under the management of Stéphane Blohorn, who has dedicated himself to restoring the firm's reputation. The location I visited, in the seventh arrondissement, is a pleasant shop, well run and stocked with excellent cheeses. And there's something endearing about being able to walk out of a store bearing a cheese emblazoned with the "Androuët" label.

Barthélemy: Owned by well-known *affineur* Roland Barthélemy and also located in the swanky seventh arrondissement, Barthélemy has an air of deliberate, very expensive diminutiveness coupled with rural nostalgia. Hens and chicks etched onto decorative glass panels adorn its front, while painted milk cans and sheep statuettes perch on window shelves. Inside, you stand in a line—there's no room to do anything but stand in line—that frequently stretches out to the street. The shopkeepers are knowledgeable, if somewhat hurried, and the cheeses are splendid.

Marie-Anne Cantin: This is an elegant—and quite famous—cheese shop, on a par with Barthélemy. The entryway, featuring a black awning and a round topiary in a container before a stark white façade, made me want to correct my posture and smooth my hair. Inside, cheeses are splayed artfully on mats of straw, and the space is so confined that customers and shopkeepers are forced to step around one another. Here you can get good old-fashioned snooty Parisian treatment from salespeople as elegant as the shop.

Beillevaire: Some might look askance at the inclusion of Beillevaire on a list of the best Parisian cheese shops: the company has multiple franchises in western France and nine locations in Paris alone. But if you're new to French cheese and want a place that is perhaps a tad more foreigner-friendly, Beillevaire is a good option. The store I know, just up the street from Barthélemy, is airy and well stocked with quality cheeses. And the helpful staff won't mind if you stand around hemming and hawing as you try to make a selection. They might even try to speak with you in English.

Pascal Trotté: One of the wonderful things about Paris is that you can be just walking down the street and stumble upon a marvelous neighborhood cheese shop such as Pascal Trotté. I happened to stop in on Christmas Eve, when the owner, who explained that his son was about to leave for the holiday, was quite gaily indulging in a tipple of champagne. I left with a smile on my face and half a wheel of Raclette.

La Fromagerie: This is where I go to buy cheese in Paris. The reddish-orange façade is located on rue Cler, a lovely little market street not far from the Eiffel Tower in the seventh arrondissement, and the store emits a marvelous barnyard scent. It stocks a fabulous array of cheeses fanned behind glass cases and stacked on shelves. Countertops hold earthenware crocks of *fromage blanc,* and if you ask for butter, one of the brisk but amiable attendants bustling about in white coats will grab a wire and cut you a slab from a huge, gleaming hunk. The only drawback of La Fromagerie is that you may be forced to assert yourself in the crowd of *grandes dames* who arrow in from both the "in" and "out" sides of the store and display the traditional French tendency to ignore what our British friends might term polite rules of queuing. But if you know anything about food in France, you know that the quality of stores across the country can be judged roughly by the demographic they attract: always go for the place with the line of little old ladies.

FROMAGESPEAK

Once you're at one of the Parisian cheese shops listed in the previous section, some of the following terms may come in handy.

affinage (af-fee-NAH-juh): the amount of time a cheese is aged.

affineur (af-fee-NUR): a professional cheese ager.

alpage (al-PAH juh): high-mountain chalet used in the Alps during the summer months to make cheese.

brebis (BRUH-bee): sheep—both the animal and the cheese, though *la brebis* is the mamma sheep (a ewe) that makes milk, while *le brebis* is the *fromage*. The generic word for "sheep" in French is *mouton,* and is usually used to refer to sheep raised for their meat.

bûche (BOOSHH): a log, but also any cheese in the shape of a log. Sainte Maure de Touraine is a *chèvre* that comes in a *bûche*. Other log-shaped goat's-milk cheeses might simply be labeled "Bûche."

carré(e) (car-AY): "square" in French, along with a host of related meanings—in terms of cheese, any square *fromage* might be casually referred to as a *carré,* even if the actual name is different. The same goes for *pavé,* after a square paving stone (although, if you see a *pavé* listed among the meat offerings at a restaurant, this refers to a hunk of steak).

chèvre (SHEV-ruh): goat—both the animal and the cheese, though *la chèvre* is the mamma goat that makes milk, while *le chèvre* is the *fromage.*

croûte (crewt): rind—literal translation is "crust." Used in French not only to describe the rind, or surface, of a cheese, but also as the word for "scab." Yummy.

croûte fleurie (crewt flew-REE): a "flowered rind"—i.e., a rind on which a coating of mold is allowed to flourish, such as with Camembert.

croûte lavée (crewt lah-VAY): a "washed rind"—i.e., a rind that is regularly brushed with brine, sometimes combined with alcohol such as *marc,* during the aging process. Many monastery cheeses fall into this category, and washed-rind cheeses are usually the ones you can smell coming.

dégustation (day-GOO-stah-syohn): a tasting, of wine or cheeses or any other gustatory delicacy, in which the point is to make comparisons.

estive (es-STEVE): high-summer cheesemaking pastures. This is essentially the generic term—related to *estival(e),* meaning "summery"—though it tends to get used more in the Pyrenees and central France.

faisselle (fay-SELL): specialized term for a cheese mold, as opposed to the generic *moule.* A fresh cheese is often sold as *une faisselle.*

fermier (fair-MYAY): farmer, as in *fromage fermier,* or "farmhouse cheese." As the name suggests, a *fermier* cheese is made on the farm, or in a small-scale setting such as an *alpage.* Some AOC cheeses can be *industriel,* but the labels for the two types are usually different, so that the consumer can tell who is being supported by the sale of the cheese.

fromage (fro-MAH-juh): cheese. I'm assuming anyone reading this book has already picked up on what this term means. You will, however, note that cheese is masculine (*le* as opposed to *la*). When in France, you must be careful, though, as some proper names for cheese are feminine. If you ask for, say, Mimolette, you need to ask for *la* Mimolette. In other words, depending on whether you're using the common or proper name, the gender of the cheese switches. Don't you just love French?

fromage de brebis (fro-MAGE duh BRUH-bee): sheep's-milk cheese.

fromage de chèvre (fro-MAGE duh SHEV-ruh): goat's-milk cheese.

fromager/fromagère (fro-mage-JAY/fro-mage-JAIR): male cheesemaker/female cheesemaker.

fourme (foorm): the generic word for "shape," but also the name of a family of cheeses in the Massif Central.

goût (goo): taste (n). See also *dégustation*.

laiterie (LAY-ta-ree): a dairy. Many artisanal cheeses in France are produced by a *laiterie,* which has a mechanized production larger than that of a farmhouse, but typically isn't as large (or impersonal) as a much larger, industrial cheese factory. The production of many AOC cheeses is split between *fermier* and *laiterie,* though some are also produced industrially.

marc (mark): a clear, colorless fruit brandy, or *eau de vie,* made from fermenting pomace, the stems, skins, and other solid bits of grapes that are left over after wine pressing. Some rind-washed cheeses are bathed in *marc* during the ripening process.

meule (muhl): a grindstone or whetstone, so a cheese in this shape— i.e., a large, heavy, round wheel. Comté comes in *meules.*

morge (MOR-juh): a mixture of water, salt, and cheese scrapings that encourages good bacterial growth, used to "wash" the exterior of certain cheeses during ripening.

paille (pie): straw. The goat cheese Sainte Maure de Touraine comes with a piece of *paille* down its middle. In former times, many cheeses were aged on mats of *paille;* some, such as St. Nectaire *fermier,* still are.

pâte (pat): the interior of the cheese; in a hard cheese, the part you eat once you've cut away the rind. In English, this is usually translated as "paste."

pâte cuite (pat qweet): "cooked" *pâte*—i.e., a cheese that is heated during the fabrication process, such as Beaufort.

pâte molle (pat moll): soft *pâte*—i.e., a cheese with a soft inside, such as Camembert. These cheeses ripen from the outside in, which is why when you cut into them, there is often a layer of creamy squishiness near the rind, while the middle may still be solid.

pâte pressée (pat PRAY-SAY): pressed *pâte*—i.e., a cheese that has been pressed but not "cooked" during fabrication, such as a *tomme*. Bear in mind that a cheese such as Beaufort has also been pressed, but because it is both pressed and cooked, it is considered a *pâte cuite.*

raclette (RACK-lette): both a cheese (Raclette) and a dish that features the cheese. The dish, in which the cheese is melted using a special machine, is traditionally served with boiled potatoes and an assortment of cornichons, pickled onions, and dried meat.

saumure (so-MUUR): water mixed with salt. Cheeses are sometimes submerged in this salt bath as part of the aging process.

souche (sue-shh): strain of bacteria. Often used to talk about different strains of *Penicillium roqueforti* in blue cheeses.

vache (vashh): a cow. You can also use this as an exclamation in French: *"Oh, la vache!"* which is roughly akin to saying "Holy cow!" in English. One of my favorite French expressions.

vacherin (VASH-ran): a cow's-milk cheese from the mountainous southeastern border of France, notably near Switzerland. The most celebrated *vacherin* is Vacherin de Haut-Doubs, also known as Mont d'Or.

SELECTED FAVORITE CHEESE BOOKS

Androuët, Pierre. *The Complete Encyclopedia of French Cheese*. Much of Androuët's cheese catalogue is now hopelessly outdated, but the introductory material is priceless and often unintentionally comic, particularly in its overly quaint English-language edition.

Boisard, Pierre. *Camembert: A National Myth*. You can't claim to be a true Camembert fanatic unless you've read this book. Seriously.

Courtine, Robert. *Larousse des fromages*. Courtine is now nearly as well known for his anti-Semitism as for his gastronomic writings. Even so, this 1970s edition remains a gold mine of *fromage* factoids. Alas, to my knowledge, it's available only in French. If you happen to know French, however, and should happen upon one, grab it. You'll be able to amaze dinner party guests for decades.

Jenkins, Steven. *Cheese Primer*. A knowledgeable guide that covers not only French cheese, but also cheeses around the world. A new edition would be nice. Still, Jenkins is a recognized expert cheesemonger and much of the info remains pertinent.

Kindstedt, Paul. *Cheese and Culture: A History of Cheese and Its Place in Western Civilization*. A thorough, scholarly, yet quite readable account of the development of cheese, from its murky beginnings to the present day. For the ardent cheese enthusiast who wants to know everything there is to know about cheese.

Masui, Kazuko, Tomoko Yamada, and Randolph Hodgson (consultant). *Dorling Kindersley French Cheeses: A Visual Guide to More Than 350 Cheeses from Every Region of France.* This is still my favorite guide to French cheese in terms of pictures. The authors managed to dig up quite a number of rather obscure *fromages,* but even with the confusion of great numbers, this guide is a must for the drool-worthy pics.

Rance, Patrick. *The French Cheese Book.* There's likely far more information here than the casual cheese lover wants, and Rance has an unfortunate tendency to recite in numbing thoroughness the litany of counts and dukes, etc., that each and every French province has known throughout the ages, but it remains the definitive English-language text on French cheese. Since it's both out of print and the object of cult-like devotion among cheese professionals, copies can be tough to find.

Robb, Graham. *The Discovery of France: A Historical Geography from the Revolution to the First World War.* Not a cheese book, but a wonderful resource for those wishing to better understand the myriad *pays* from which the cheeses of France spring.

Thorpe, Liz. *The Cheese Chronicles: A Journey Through the Making and Selling of Cheese in America, from Field to Farm to Table.* If you want to know the best places to find the best American producers making French-style cheeses (which, really, is the most environmentally sound way to get your cheese), this is the book for you. Thorpe shows that although France may be "the Mother Ship," America's up-and-coming *fromagers* and *fromagères* ain't no slouches, either.

NOTES

For the purposes of narrative and logic, the order in which chapters appear in this book does not necessarily reflect the order in which I conducted research—for example, the visit to the Chambon *buron* which leads off the book was, in fact, the last site visit I undertook.

All conversions from the metric system are approximate. All translations from the original French, oral or written, are the author's own unless otherwise noted. In an attempt to preserve the flavor of the original, particularly in regards to speech, translations are often literal. Where warranted, however, I have tried to give a sense of the meaning behind the speaker's words rather than a direct, literal translation. In the interests of time and logic, I have also sometimes collapsed and/ or rearranged speech—for example, I've taken sentences gleaned from various times during an hour-and-a-half-long interview and put them together in the same paragraph. In all cases I have done my utmost to ensure that this process does not result in connotations unintended by the original speaker.

A CHEESEHEAD CONFRONTS PARADISE

2 **china banded in moss green and gilt:** Site visit, Château de Valençay, March 35, 2008. Other details used to create the scene also come from artifacts I saw at the château; whether or not these might have been used during a visit by Napóleon, I do not know.

5 **bizarre, alien yellow:** The inventor of the Cheesehead, Ralph Bruno, explains that the cheese the Cheeseheads are modeled on "does not exist." Quoted in Jerry Apps, *Cheese: The Making of a Wisconsin Tradition* (Amherst, WI: Amherst Press, 1998), p. 173.

5 **invented in Colby, Wisconsin:** Several sources state that Colby was the first new cheese invented in the United States, in 1874, but others claim that the cheese factory where it would have been invented did not go into production until 1882.

6 *New York Times* **report:** Monica Davey, "Wisconsin's Crown of Cheese Is Within California's Reach," *New York Times,* September 30, 2006. Quotes which follow are from the article.

6 **"Cheese is a kind of secular religion":** James Norton, "Hold the Cream of Mushroom Soup: Upper Midwestern Fare Goes Highend," Chow.com, October 6, 2006.

7 **not really cheese at all:** Kraft has gotten into hot water for its "real cheese" claims. Look on a package of Mac & Cheese and you will note that the sauce packet contains "whey, salt, milk, skim milk, milk fat and milk protein concentrate," followed by "less than 2%" of a bunch of nearly unpronounceable substances. It might taste a bit like cheese, but true cheese (as American cheese expert and author Liz Thorpe often notes) is made with three basic ingredients: milk, rennet, and salt.

8 **a rate of five million kilos a year:** "Roquefort: Garanti d'Origine et de Qualité." Brochure conçue et réalisée par la Confédération Générale des Producteurs de lait de brebis et des Industriels de Roquefort (Millau), pp. 11–12.

8 **"showed the path":** Hervé Mons, quoted in "Pierre Androuët: La mort d'un guide," *Profession Fromager: Le magazine des fromages de tradition,* 16 (March–April 2005), pp. 4–11. This and quotes immediately following are from the article.

9 **alongside dog food and shoelaces:** William Grimes, "Patrick Rance, 81, British Cheese Crusader," *New York Times,* August 30, 1999.

9 **"but life is too short":** Patrick Rance, *The French Cheese Book* (London: Macmillan, 1989), p. xix.

9 **"the best of all":** Egan Ronay, "Major Patrick Rance: Gentleman responsible for the creation of Britain's farm cheese industry," Guardian.co.uk, August 31, 1999.

10 **"turned into full-spectrum color":** Cynthia Zarin, "Big Cheese: The Village Landmark That Helped Put Cheese on the Map Is Making a Move," *The New Yorker,* August 23, 2004, p. 40.

10 **"nowhere like France":** Liz Thorpe, *The Cheese Chronicles: A Journey Through the Making and Selling of Cheese in America, from Field to Farm to Table* (New York: Ecco, 2009), p. 180. This and subsequent quote.

11 **"an act of murder":** Pierre Androuët, *The Complete Encyclopedia of French Cheese and Many Other Continental Varieties,* trans. John Githens (New York: Harper's Magazine Press, 1973), p. 30.

13 **girdled by a strip of spruce bark:** Technically speaking, this is the inner layer of tree bark known as the "cambium" and not the outer, rougher layer. In France, the people who harvest the strips—"*les sangles*"—are known as *sangliers*. Such harvesting is an artisan trade unto itself.

14 **"as worthy of preserving as a sixteenth-century building":** Carolo Petrini, quoted in Barrie Kerper, *Southwest France: The Collected Traveler* (New York: Fodor's, 2003), p. 99.

CHAPTER 1: DREAM A LITTLE DREAM OF CHEESE

17 *département*: roughly equivalent to a U.S. county.

17 **"no substitute for doing it the old-fashioned way"**: Max Mc-Calman and David Gibbons, *The Cheese Plate* (New York: Clarkson Potter, 2002), pp. 33–34.

19 **a cartographer trying to survey the land was hacked to death**: Graham Robb, *The Discovery of France: A Historical Geography from the Revolution to the First World War* (New York, London: W. W. Norton, 2007): p. 3.

19 **"can remain out of range of a rifle"**: Quoted in ibid., p. 5.

20 **family of cylindrical mountain cheeses known as *fourmes***: Robert J. Courtine, *Larousse des fromages* (Paris: Librairie Larousse, 1973), p. 103. Courtine explains that "*fourme*" is the "*nom générique de nombreux fromages montagnards du centre de la France.*" This would include the blue cheese Fourme d'Ambert, which though considerably smaller, has the beer-keg shape typical of all *fourmes*.

23 **fewer than a half dozen still make cheese**: Deffontaines, *Salers, un produit, un paysage.* (Paris: Les Éditions de l'Épure, 2007), p. 30.

24 **17,000 tons of Cantal**: Deffontaines, *Salers,* p. 7.

25 **"all summer long, for fifteen years"**: Liz Thorpe, "Making Mons," April 4, 2006, bigcheesestories.blogspot.com. Quotes are from her blog post.

26 **over 75 percent butterfat**: Though this percentage sounds alarming, it's not as bad as you might think. The cheese is largely water and technically speaking, the fat is 75 percent of the dry matter in the cheese.

26 ***Ces fromages qu'on assassine***: Joël Santoni, prod. Jean-Charles Deniau (Paris: Panama Productions/France 3, Bo Films, 2007), DVD. Subsequent quotes from film.

26 **inspired by the Franco–American documentary *Mondovino*:** *"Ces Fromages Qu'on Assassine . . . Qui lait cru?"* leblogtvnews.com.

31 **a health official claimed:** *Sentinelles des montagnes: Les Burons de l'Aubrac, des monts du Cantal et du Cézallier* (Parc Saint-Joseph: Éditions du Rouergue, 2008), p. 92.

40 **entire hand-milking was staged:** In defense of Hervé Mons and the cheesemakers at the Taillé *buron*, it's possible they were not aware how the footage they participated in filming would be presented by the filmmakers. For example, one of the scientists at INRA-Poligny, Eric Beuvier, was visibly upset at how INRA's research had been portrayed. "The journalists were dishonest," he told me. "I didn't know they had an axe to grind."

CHAPTER 2: THE DILEMMA OF MILK

In this chapter I owe a debt of gratitude to Harold McGee's always superlative *On Food and Cooking* for its clear and comprehensible explanations of the cheesemaking process. I am also thankful for Graham Robb's terrific *The Discovery of France* for enlarging my understanding of how France and its peoples evolved.

44 **A recipe you can make at home:** McCalman and Gibbons, *The Cheese Plate,* p. 41.

48 **liquid had somehow transformed into chunky, edible white stuff:** One French cheese historian, Michel Bouvier, thinks it's also likely ancient peoples discovered cheese by noticing the curds in the stomachs of young animals killed while hunting. Cheese historian Paul Kindstedt further notes that since most adult humans at the time would have been lactose intolerant, and therefore would not have drunk milk, the legend is indeed very likely just a legend.

49 **cheese made from reindeer milk:** Michel Bouvier, *Le fromage c'est toute une histoire (*Paris: Jean-Paul Rocher, 2008), p. 7.

49 **go dry if milked in anything but complete silence:** Carmen Nobel, "Moody Moose Make $420 Cheese: Big Spender," The Street.com.

50 **"creature of the breast" . . . allows our brains to keep developing:** Harold McGee, *On Food and Cooking: The Science and Lore of the Kitchen* (New York: Scribner, 1984), pp. 7–8.

50 **"You think this is ridiculous? It is":** Rory Freedman and Kim Barnouin, *Skinny Bitch: A No-Nonsense, Tough-Love Guide for Savvy Girls Who Want to Stop Eating Crap and Start Looking Fabulous!* (Philadelphia: Running Press, 2005), pp. 55–59.

50 **enough calcium for thirty:** J. E. Umphrey and C. R. Staples, "General Anatomy of Ruminant Digestive System," University of Florida/IFAS Extension, edis.ifas.ufl.edu.

53 **like a melting Wendy's Frosty:** "Inside the Cow's Stomach," awp. diaart.org/dunning/cowstomach.

54 **90 percent of French and Germans, 40 percent of:** McGee, *On Food and Cooking,* p. 10.

54 **7,000-year-old cave art:** Cynthia Clampitt, "Yes, Sir, Cheese My Baby," *Hungry Magazine,* March 20, 2008.

54 **archaeological sites in Burgundy and the French Jura:** Bouvier, *Le fromage,* p. 10.

54 **4,500-year-old mosaic from Mesopotamia:** Ibid., p. 19.

54 **traces of real cheese dating to Egypt's first dynastic period:** Ibid., p. 11.

55 **cheeses in ancient times would have been relatively rudimentary:** The technology for making cheese with rennet may, in fact, have taken some time to develop. According to Paul Kindstedt, the first definitive evidence for rennet use is to be found in Hittite texts from around 1400 BCE.

57 **devised a system for classifying cheeses:** Claire Delfosse, *La France Fromagère* (Paris: La Boutique de l'Histoire Éditions, 2007), p. 44. Note: his system apparently didn't contain the further refinement for *pâtes molles*.

58 **one for each finger:** I'm admittedly leaving cheeses made from whey—what are called "lactoserum" cheeses—off this list. The process of making them is quite different: they "precipitate" out of leftover whey. The most familiar whey cheese is likely ricotta, though the French can claim one as well. Called Brocciu, it's made on Corsica, though one Corsican cheesemaker told me "it's not really cheese." Also, although you'll often see goat cheeses put in their own category, they actually all fall into one of the main categories. The only difference is that they're made with goat's milk rather than cow's. The same goes for sheep's-milk cheeses. It ought to be further borne in mind that most *bleus* are also considered soft cheeses—*pâtes molles*—it's just that they're blue soft cheeses.

58 **monasteries became sanctums of cheese knowledge:** In addition to improving cheese technology, monks were also instrumental in clearing a great deal of pasture lands.

58 **the Hittites even placated weather gods:** Paul S. Kindstedt, *Cheese and Culture: A History of Cheese and Its Place in Western Civilization* (White River Junction, VT: Chelsea Green Publishing, 2012), p. 44.

60 **and the monks like to joke that the notes sink down:** I can't claim originality for this image. In *The Cheese Nun,* Mother Marcellino talks about the cheeses listening to the monks singing.

60 **"lay fallen about the round on the grey-veined marble":** Sylvie Girard, *Le Monde des fromages* (Paris: Hatier, 1994), p. 32.

61 **"Was it supposed":** Rance, *The French Cheese Book,* p. 348.

61 **enzymes produced by the bacteria:** See McGee's *On Food and Cooking,* pp. 59–63.

63 **tax of one Maroilles cheese per cow per year:** *Sur les traces de l'abbaye de Maroilles: Circuit à parcourir à pied,* booklet produced by the Parc Naturel Régional de l'Avesnois, p. 6.

64 **Maroilles could even be personalized:** Rance, *The French Cheese Book,* p. 259.

64 **one day Charlemagne stopped:** This anecdote is the subject of much dispute. There is some uncertainty about which abbey exactly hosted the monarch. The biography of Charlemagne in which the story appears does not specify the place, and some historians seem to have assumed it was the Abbey de Vabre (which is much closer to the *caves*). Additionally, Paul Kindstedt writes that even the type of cheese is ambiguous in the original, and therefore it cannot be said with any certainly it was Roquefort. Whatever the case may be, Conques does appear to have supplied the king with Roquefort—though one French source says they were sending it to him out of gratitude for the famous A-shaped reliquary he bestowed on Conques.

66 **"*Non au fromage à la vache!*":** Sign 2 on the self-guided walking tour of the Parc Naturel Régional de l'Avesnois, site visit, Maroilles, September 16, 2008.

67 **If trees were sparse in the hills:** In visiting various regions, it seemed evident to me that "cooking" became the method of choice in the Alps and the Jura because cheesemaking structures were located either in or close to trees, and that it was not used in regions such as the Massif Central because of the relative lack of trees. In the Alps, cows are often pastured above tree line (but even so the chalets

are at or below tree line), while in the Jura there is very little land above tree line at all. In the Massif Central, meanwhile, though there are lots of trees, *burons*, as I have noted elsewhere, were nearly always in the midst of quite large patches of cleared land. Claude Querry, of the *caves* at St. Antoine, confirmed my hypothesis and reports that Hervé Mons also shares this view.

68 **outnumbering human newborns ten to one:** From signage at site visit, Thônes Co-op de Reblochon, June 2007.

69 **vision of satanic demons:** Cabécou du Périgord website, history section, www.cabecou-perigord.com/histoire.

69 **"spheres of audible influence":** Robb, *The Discovery of France,* p. 30. This and quotes that immediately follow.

CHAPTER 3: A LITTLE GOAT CHEESE

72 **"get to the suckling babies faster":** Jean Froc, *Balade au pays des fromages: Les traditions fromagères en France* (Versailles: Éditions Quæ, 2006), p. 16.

72 **your goat wet nurse directly to the doorsteps of city dwellers:** Ibid., p. 16.

77 **that would affect him for the rest of his life:** Personal interview with Isabelle Androuët, June 2011.

79 **the establishment's *livre d'or*:** Ibid.

87 **"not so much a moveable as a moving feast":** Rance, *The French Cheese Book,* p. 472.

88 **"they looked like horse dung":** Rance, *The French Cheese Book,* p. 66.

90 **Law for the Protection of the Place:** In French, the *"Loi du 6 mai 1919 rèlative à la protection des appellations d'origine."* I've also seen this translated as the "Act of 6 May 1919 on the protection of AOCs."

92 **"made using traditional savoir faire":** Suzanne Kestenberg, "50 questions sur les produits laitiers," *Vie Pratique Santé*, no. 15 (28 février–26 mars 2008).

CHAPTER 4: CHEESE IS A BATTLEFIELD

I am highly indebted throughout this chapter to Pierre Boisard's superb and exhaustively researched *Camembert: A National Myth* (trans. Richard Miller. Berkeley: University of California Press, 2003). The book greatly expanded my understanding both of the history of Camembert and its fabrication, and many of my descriptions of both rely on Boisard's work.

101 **"all because of profit":** Elaine Sciolino, "If Rules Change, Will Camembert Stay the Same?" *New York Times*, June 20, 2007.

102 **"had the same circular shape":** Pierre Boisard, *Camembert: A National Myth*, trans. Richard Miller (Berkeley: University of California Press, 2003), p. 113.

104 **passing it from mother to daughter:** Ibid., p. 54.

104 **long-standing tradition of cheese espionage:** Ibid., p. 56.

106 **Dapper in a check suit and carrying a cardboard suitcase:** This, at least, is how he is pictured in Gérard Roger's book *La Fabuleuse histoire du Camembert* (Vimoutiers: Normandie Plus, 1991).

108 **with miniature versions of the American and French flags:** Boisard, *Camembert*, p. 4.

108 **was not invented out of whole cloth by the Norman cheesemakers:** Ibid., p. 204.

109 **kneeling to pray at the foot of her statue:** Ibid., p. 26.

110 **"according to one's tastes and fantasies":** Ibid., p. 218. This and quotes that immediately follow.

110 **"It will be sharp":** Androuët, *The Complete Encyclopedia of French Cheese and Many Other Continental Varieties,* p. 31.

111 **"divining a fromage is a little bit like alchemy":** Courtine, *Larousse des fromages,* p. 71.

115 **"four techniques":** The different pasteurization methods might be summarized (with some help from Harold McGee) as follows: In "pasteurization," also known as high-temperature, short-time (HTST) pasteurization, the temperature is at least 161°F and the time at least fifteen seconds. In "thermalization," also known as "vat" or "batch" pasteurization, the temperature is a minimum of 145°F and the time at least thirty minutes. Harold McGee further notes: "The batch process has a relatively mild effect on flavor, while the HTST method is hot enough to denature around 10% of the whey proteins and generate the strongly aromatic gas hydrogen sulfide. Though this 'cooked' flavor was considered a defect in the early days, U.S. consumers have come to expect it, and dairies now often intensify it by pasteurizing at well above the minimum temperature; 171°F is commonly used."

117 **Throughout these stages:** These descriptions of the travails of the Camembert making process rely on information found in Pierre Boisard's book.

118 **Cyrille alone churned out 150,000 rounds:** Boisard, *Camembert,* p. 52.

118 **"thereby enlarging its circle of admirers":** Boisard, *Camembert,* p. 79.

120 **heating milk coagulated its proteins:** Boisard, *Camembert,* p. 164.

121 **some 831 illnesses, 66 hospitalizations, and one death:** www .foodsafety.ksu.edu, RawMilkOutbreakTable.

121 **raw-milk black market:** Joe Drape, "Should This Milk be Legal?" *New York Times,* August 8, 2007.

121 **begin thermalizing their milk as a preventive measure:** Vacherin Mont d'Or, Patrimoine Culinaire Suisse, www.kulinaris cheserbe.ch.

122 **"trying to get at us at the dining table":** Boisard, *Camembert,* p. 220.

126 **left to bear the Camembert mantle alone:** Rance does note that there was apparently a neighbor also making *fermier* Camembert at the time of this visit; I assume that this person subsequently gave up. Also, though Nadia said François's father did not make Camembert, Rance identifies La Héronnière as the farm of Robert Durand. Presumably François was even then in charge of cheesemaking though he had not yet taken over the family business.

131 **keeping that milk raw is likely the best way:** French defenders of cheese quite rightly note that consumption of raw-milk cheeses is at shockingly low levels; in France they account for only about 4 percent of the total cheese market. That said, figures supplied by the Conseil National des Appellations d'Origine Laitières show that sales of raw milk cheese actually rose by 2.6 percent in 2009, even with the financial crisis.

CHAPTER 5: HIGH ON A HILL

134 **nearly 150 pounds:** Official AOC statistics put the weight of a Beaufort at twenty to seventy kilograms, with an average weight between forty and forty-five kilograms at the end of *affinage.*

139 **In the area patois:** Another patois word connected with the origin of the Reblochon name is *reblasser,* which means "to pilfer." Robert Courtine thought both could be applicable, and that perhaps *reblasser*

led to *reblocher,* which led to "Reblochon," because a second milking could be considered pilfering in any case.

142 **originally came from around the town of Gruyères:** Although *gruyère* lore cites this town as the birthplace of the cheeses, cheese historian Paul Kindstedt notes that the technology for "cooking" cheeses in order to remove more whey was, in fact, likely based on methods developed by Celtic people. It's possible the Celts had a hand in developing the other main technology for removing enough whey to make a large-format cheese: the process of grinding and salting used for *fourmes.*

142 ***grueries* were managed by an agent *gruyer*:** Michel Vernus and Daniel Greusard, *Le pays des fromages: La Franche-Comté* (Joué-lès-Tours: Éditions Alan Sutton, 2001).

142 **most *gruyères* in France are called something else:** This is true even though the official names of many French *gruyères* still contain the word (e.g., Gruyère de Beaufort).

143 **"give a certain addictive quality to these foods":** Neal Barnard, quoted in "Break Food Seduction," www.healthscience.org.

144 **"you might call it dairy crack":** Neal Barnard, quoted in "Cheese Contains Morphine," www.care2.com.

146 **"they give no milk for forty-eight hours":** Rance, *The French Cheese Book,* p. 146.

146 **cows that are given names turn out to be better milkers:** Newcastle University study. Various Web sources reported on the findings, which originally appeared in *Anthrozoos: Journal of the International Society for Anthrozoology.* See, for example, www.scientistlive.com/European-Food-Scientist/Technology/Happy_cows_produce_more_milk.

148   **billions of bacteria:** I do not exaggerate. There are reportedly 500,000 billion bacteria and 50 billion protozoa to be found in a cow's digestive system.

149   **"thirty-six plant species":** Rance, *The French Cheese Book,* p. 422.

153   **figure fell to 7 percent:** Guy R. Mermier, *France: Past and Present* (New York: Peter Lang, 2000), p. 170.

153   **better living sweeping chimneys in Paris:** Julie Deffontaines, *Beaufort, un produit, un paysage* (Paris: Les Éditions de l'Épure, 2004), p. 8.

154   **fallen to a scant five hundred tons a year:** Deffontaines, *Beaufort, un produit, un paysage,* p. 8.

154   **Viallet was on hand to present the pontiff:** "Anecdote sur le Pape et le Beaufortain," territoire.lebeaufortain.com.

155   **deemed too industrial to be shown:** Interestingly, the film does show the *machines à traire* in the Alps; presumably the role of the machines there is so well known that any attempt to hide them would have been ridiculous.

159   **less than 6 percent:** Deffontaines, *Beaufort, un produit, un paysage,* p. 5.

159   **today there are only a dozen:** Roland Barthélemy and Arnaud Sperat-Czar, *Guide du fromage* (Hachette Pratique, 2003).

CHAPTER 6: BIG FRUIT

161   **stuck on the threshold for two days:** Michel Vernus, *Le Comté: Une saveur venue des siècles,* excerpt found on signboard at the Hameau du Fromage, Cléron.

165   **40 percent of French households eat Comté:** Rance, *The French Cheese Book,* p. 395.

166 **"Robotic artisan cheesemaking is an oxymoron!":** Francis Percival, "Robots Take a Turn," *Culture: The Word on Cheese* (Winter 2010).

168 **celebration in the nearby town of Montlebon:** The French version of Wikipedia does make it plain that the Retour des Alpages is a "folkloric" festival because "there haven't been any *alpages* in the Morteau valley for decades." This of course suggests that there were some at some point, an assertion I can neither confirm nor deny.

170 **"the same bread and the same pot":** Vernus and Greusard, *Le pays des fromages,* p. 19.

170 **buildings catching fire from the huge flames:** Ibid., p. 23.

173 **poets composed songs about them:** Ibid., p. 25.

178 **they're judged by the *affineurs* on a scale of one to twenty:** Kazuko Masui, Tomoko Yamada, and Randolph Hodgson (consultant), *Dorling Kindersley French Cheeses* (London: Dorling Kindersley, 1996), p. 113.

178 **a jury of professionals meets regularly:** www.comte.com.

179 **a picture of a "*superbe*" round:** Vernus and Greusard, *Le pays des fromages,* pp. 39–41.

179 **aren't supposed to have much in the way of eyes:** Authors Michel Vernus and Daniel Greusard explain that the loss of eyes in Comté may also be because cows are now milked under far more hygienic conditions and the milk stays much cleaner—which means fewer hole-making microscopic beasties.

180 **people were asked to follow a trail of chocolate essential oil:** Noam Sobel and Rehan M. Khan, "How the Nose Knows What It Knows," *Nature Neuroscience* 10, no. 7 (January 1, 2007).

CHAPTER 7: BASTARD CAVES AND ROTTEN BREAD

185 **"badass environmentalist":** Florence Williams, "The Roquefort Files," *Outside,* June 2001. Subsequent quotes describing the assault on the Millau McDonald's are also from this article.

186 **"the symbol of the standardization of food":** Quoted in ibid.

187 **a tour kicked off:** Site visit, *caves* at Société, October 4, 2008.

189 **Société owns 90 percent:** Julie Deffontaines, *Roquefort: Un produit, un paysage.* (Paris: Les Éditions de l'Épure, 2005), p. 22.

191 **remnants of 2,700-year-old molds for shaping cheese:** "L'histoire du Roquefort en quelques dates," www.roquefort-societe.com.

193 **then they're ready for the *piquage*:** This, at least, is the general Roquefort-making process. The methods of each maker vary; Patrick Rance gives extensive descriptions of different methods in *The French Cheese Book.*

193 **Roussel, of the village of Laqueuille:** Rance says that Roussel was from Villeviale, between Rochefort and Laqueuille, though his reference is the only one of its type I've come across. All the other sources I've consulted, including the French ones, state that Roussel was from Laqueuille.

193 **"applied himself during long months":** Froc, *Balade au pays des fromages,* pp. 136–37.

195 **"when no sap is rising":** Rance, *The French Cheese Book,* p. 190.

195 **or about 750 a day:** Site visit, *caves* at Société, October 4, 2008.

196 **is a Roquefort sheep farmer:** It's interesting to note that the Glandièreses' house and sheep farm is located at the edge of Sainte-Eulalie-de-Cernon, one of a chain of five strongholds built in the Roquefort area by the Templars in the twelfth century. Under what

one French source terms the *"réglementation draconienne"* of this militaristic order, area peasants increased their flocks and were forced to strictly manage pastures. Paul Kindstedt writes that the influence of the Templars, along with that of the Benedictine and Cistercian monastic orders in the Roquefort trade, gave the cheese added repute and may have helped lead to the first, rudimentary *appellation d'origine* granted in 1411.

197 **is so expensive:** Lacaune milk production, in spite of being high compared to yesteryear, is still about half of what an East Friesian— the dairy sheep breed of choice in the United States—produces.

197 **average was 14:** Charles Blondeau, *Les caves de Roquefort* (1877; reprint, Nîmes: Lacour Éditeur, 1999), p. 12.

200 **more than 1,100 locations:** Edward Cody, "Le Sandwich Takes a Bite Out of French Tradition," *Washington Post,* June 26, 2009.

200 **70 in Paris alone:** Hugo Rifkind, "Supersize . . . Moi? How the French Learnt to Love McDonald's," TimesOnline, August 19, 2008.

200 **revenue in France rose 11 percent:** Ibid.

201 *cabanières* **composed 90 percent:** Maurice Labbé and Jean-Pierre Serres, *Mémoire en images: Roquefort en Aveyron* (Saint-Cyr-sur-Loire: Alan Sutton, 2002), p. 76.

202 **"une énorme machine industrielle et commerciale":** Delfosse, *La France Fromagère,* p. 163.

203 **the cheese itself became more and more standardized:** Ibid., p. 164.

203 **Hence the United States' sixty-day rule:** Ibid., p. 175.

204 **considerably higher in fat, sodium, and cholesterol:** Nutrition Data.com.

CHAPTER 8: THE OLD SHEEPHERDER

206 **"the size and sex of a straying beast":** Rance, *The French Cheese Book*, p. 131.

208 **for some four thousand years:** Ibid., p. 131.

211 **"both were composers":** Ibid., p. 135.

215 **stone-and-mortar *cabane*:** These were traditionally called *kayolars* or *cayolars*, though when I asked René, he said they just called them *cabanes*. Roland Barthélemy also gives *etchola*, a Basque word, as a synonym.

221 **nearly half the European Union's total expenditures:** Doreen Carvajal and Stephen Castle, "European Subsidies Stray from the Farm," *New York Times*, July 16, 2009.

222 **85 percent of aid goes to a 17 percent sliver:** Jack Thurston, "Le Monde debates the CAP," February 1, 2010, capreform.eu.

222 **over half a million dollars for his French wheat farms:** Carvajal and Castle, "European Subsidies Stray."

226 **Auvergne's proximity to ancient salt routes:** Kindstedt, *Cheese and Culture*, p. 107.

226 **ten million square meters:** Alain Marnezy and Noël Martin, "La tempête des 7–8 Novembre 1982 dans le département de l'Isère," www.persee.fr.

227 **"A living tradition":** Boisard, *Camembert*, p. 191.

CODA: *JOYEUSES* CHEESE FÊTES

232 **"running with wine and Livarot":** Peter Mayle, *French Lessons: Adventures with Knife, Fork, and Corkscrew* (New York: Knopf, 2001), p. 87.

232 **The Grand Master:** Personal interview with Eric Masselier, December 3, 2008.

240 *Lingonese formaticum, formaticum lingonese*: Though the Latin word for cheese is *caseus,* the word *formaticum* was also used, probably to refer to an aged, or "formed," cheese. Hence *"Lingonese formaticum, formaticum lingonese"* roughly translates to "Langres cheese, cheese of Langres."

ABOUT THE AUTHOR

A native of Wisconsin, "America's Dairyland," Kathe Lison has a long-reaching history with cheese. Her maternal grandfather kept and milked a dozen Holsteins on a sixty-acre farm north of Green Bay, and her great-great-grandfather owned a dairy. Beyond her Cheesehead lineage, Lison holds an MFA in creative nonfiction from Goucher College. She is an award-winning essayist whose work has appeared in numerous literary journals and a recipient of an Emerging Artist Grant from the Utah Arts Council. One of her essays was cited as a "Notable Essay" in *The Best American Essays 2006*. She lives in Tucson, Arizona, with her partner, science and nature writer Christopher Cokinos, and their three cats.